This book is presented to:

_____

Books
Are
Wings

LIVE UNITED
United Way

United Way of Rhode Island

D1418080

DANGEROUS BIRDS

BOOKS BY JANET LEMBKE

River Time

Looking for Eagles

JANET LEMBKE

Dangerous
Birds

A Naturalist's Aviary

LYONS & BURFORD, PUBLISHERS

Printed in the United States of America

10 9 8 7 6 5 4 3 2 1

Library of Congress Cataloging-in-Publication Data

Lembke, Janet.
Dangerous birds : a naturalist's aviary / Janet Lembke.
p.   cm.
ISBN 1-55821-190-X
1. Dangerous birds. I. Title.
QL677.75.L46   1992
598–dc20   92-18332
                                CIP

Portions of this book have appeared previously in the following magazines:

Audubon: "A Bird in the Hand"
The North American Review: "When the Wind Found Shape"
North Carolina Literary Review: "Thirteen Ways of Looking at a Grackle"
Wildlife in North Carolina: "Silence in the Winter Woods"

For my children's children
Russell, Melissa, Margaret, Hans-William, and Joseph

Contents

Acknowledgments

In addition to the there-and-then legendary and literary figures who acted as consultants for these stories, several people very much of the here and now freely contributed their knowledge, educated opinions, and highly contagious enthusiasm for everything under heaven: John Fussell, III, reliable guide to the birds of the Carolina coast; Stephanie Goetzinger, wildlife rehabilitator, director of OWLS, and advocate for a sharp-shinned hawk; John Herington, classical detective; John Mehner, keeper of doves and an altared owl; and Warren Starnes, guardian of longleaf pines and the race of kings that dwells therein. To you all, my admiration and happy thanks.

Introduction

The stories in this book deal most obviously with birds. They are meant as an aviary housing a hodgepodge of species—some that are easily seen, some that aren't, and some that can't be seen at all. Honest-to-goodness field-guide birds, the sort that can be watched with eyes, share the pages with birds that can be observed only in memory and imagination, the birds of myth and poetry, the birds of Mother Goose and Edward Lear.

But first, before my adventures with such an array of avifauna are put into geographic and temporal contexts, a confession might be in order: Given a choice between wings and a prehensile tail, I'd choose the tail. A tail is practical. Just think of its uses! They number more than Disney's hundred and one Dalmatians, more than the thousand and one tales of Scheherezade. They are as many as the fish in the ocean, the birds in the air. These days I could use a tail to give me an extra point of balance—or to swat away deerflies—while my hands hold binoculars. Once it would have helped mightily to snatch a toddler back from the brink of disaster—or to tickle a small tummy, hold a small hand. That tail would eliminate my habit of toting what my grandmother disapprovingly called a "lazy man's load," things piled in hands, in arms, under arms, under chin to such an extent that slips and spills are inevitable, and picking up the stuff takes twice the time that making two trips in the first place would have. A tail, yes! Besides, who needs wings? I already have a perfectly good pair inside my head, where they often unfold and stretch to their full span and take me anywhere I want to go.

Going somewhere—each journey has a starting point. My travels through the landscapes and centuries of observing birds usually begin in one of two quite tangible, finite, and down-to-earth places. Between them, they grant me what seems the two best of all possible worlds (though lovers of deserts might disagree): access to mountains and access to water.

The mountains are the Blue Ridge and the Western Range of the Appalachians, the wooded and worn-down limestone walls that gently guard Virginia's Shenandoah Valley. With my husband the Chief and our Doberman Sally, I spend the winter months in the Valley—to be precise, in Staunton, the small town of my growing up, population twenty thousand then and now. The seat of rural, cattle- and corn-raising Augusta County, it was first settled in the second decade of the 1700s and built upon an outcropping of steep hills—no sense in locating a town atop more level acreage that could be put to better use as farmland.

As might be expected, even such a modest city offers all the amenities for urban birds, uncountable starlings and pigeons too many to number. It also holds surprises. Fish crows have long inhabited a rookery in the yard of Trinity Church, which is now smack-dab downtown, but in colonial days it was the meeting place for

Virginia's House of Burgesses. And early one morning, two back-yards away in my Victorian neighborhood, where middle-sized houses in tiny yards rise in ranks like stair steps toward the top of a truly precipitous hill, there appeared a bird of overgrown fields and forest edges, a bird of the high Blue Ridge where it courts with whistling flights on balmy spring evenings, an altogether unexpected bird—the woodcock. And in an older, more elegant and stately neighborhood on the other side of town, I met a turkey vulture, but that's a story in itself. Nor need I leave the city limits to find other birds associated not with urban circumstances but with countryside and wilderness. Migrating waterfowl, such as oldsquaw and ruddy ducks (and once a brant), land with autumnal regularity on a park pond; grouse and wild turkeys, along with startling white-tailed deer, break from cover beside another park's woodland path.

I do leave town, of course, to drive down county roads, some still not paved even in this day and age of onrushing macadam, fast-food joints, and satellite dishes. Often, a friend and I visit the heron creeks, the redwing marshes, the hemlock ridges where flocks of golden-crowned kinglets and slow-voiced black-capped chickadees bustle and feed, the hedgerows that roil with cardinals and ever-volatile sparrows. Hoping for luck—a kestrel, a loggerhead shrike—but settling not unhappily for a mob of juncos, a slew of jays, and four species of woodpeckers, friend and I participate in the Audubon Society's annual Christmas Bird Count. Sometimes, we do get lucky: Once, in a winter-bare sapling at the foot of a railroad trestle, seven Savannah sparrows were making sport like children on a playground jungle gym; once, on an upper branch of a scrubby Virginia pine, two pine warblers perched with the utter immobility of study specimens. They were so unexpected, so out of their usual wintering grounds, that we were required to fill out a report so that our sighting could be verified—detailed description of the species, our distance from the birds and how it was estimated, the light conditions available, the manufacturer and magnification of our viewing equipment, and more, more, more, including how, precisely, we had been able to figure out just what it was that we were looking at. The answer to that question was elementary: Year-round I see pine warblers in coastal North Carolina, the other country in which my adventures begin.

Eight months of the year, with visits during the other four, the Chief, Sally, and I live in an elderly, twelve-by-sixty, quite immobile mobile home set a scant seventy-five feet back from the south bank of the wide and salty Neuse River. (The name is pronounced *noose,* but my classically tutored imagination prefers to think of it as rhyming with *Zeus.*) The place—an isolated, rural enclave ignored on all maps except the nautical chart for this stretch of river—is Great Neck Point. And along its shore, on lots that once grew corn and tobacco or supported woodlands, our habitations—trailers, cottages, an increasing number of four-square houses—rise higgledy-piggledy in an ad hoc community ungoverned by zoning codes or covenants. With its wonderfully varied assortment of habitats—river and shore, ponds, creeks, wetlands, woods, and fields—the Point has long been a paradise for birds, fish, deer, and snakes and, more recently, for people. Paradise, yes, and a focus for a certain kind of splendidly teeming disorder.

Time for a pause and another confession: I advocate untidiness. Not only advocate it, but strive to protect it in the form it takes at Great Neck Point. Let me explain. It might be accurate to call the Point a brushpile on a grand scale. Eclectically, sometimes inseparably, it jumbles together natural and human wildness. It certainly displays every emblem of human zeal and turpitude. Some residents, exhibiting passions for order and symmetry, mow lawns every other day in warm weather, hoe out vegetable-garden weeds the moment they poke green and sassy from the ground, and compost every last scrap of organic waste. Other people flaunt an absolute talent for disorder: Vegetables compete with grasses, Jimson, and bindweed for room in the gardens; foundered pickup trucks, beds laden with miscellaneous junk, are put to pasture in the yards; treadless tires are consigned to the river. Depending on the state of repair of the two local tractors, the fields may or may not be bushhogged, the dirt road may be graded or left an obstacle course of ruts and potholes. And, except to retrieve the lumber from storm-broken piers, nobody cleans up the woods and the shore. Expired trees lie where they fall; waterborne flotsam, augmented by pine straw and pine cones, collects in ridges as far inland as wind-impelled water can shove it. Mixed with the natural litter are human leavings, the predictable cans and bottles, broken boards and bits of fishing line, along with some totally unexpected offerings, such as one old blue sock and the nearly new toilet seat that someone suspended five feet off the ground on an innocent pine branch. The beach is always littered—gull feathers, crab claws, dead fish, shells that used to encase oysters or mussels, shells that used to encase birdshot or buckshot, water-rounded bits of brick, glass shards that may be as new as yesterday or predate the Revolutionary War, plastic of every conceivable chemistry, color, and configuration, and tires, ever more tires. In many respects, both human and natural, the Point looks like a dump. It's also as fully rooted in its casual disorder as the brushpile island of honeysuckle, beauty berry, and pokeweed that rises lushly out of the lake of green grass in a neighbor's field. Tidiness presents an image of sterility—the picture-perfect house in which nobody lives. Untidiness catches the eye and pricks interest. There's always something new to see, though it may be unsightly or downright dangerous—sowbugs beneath that old blue sock, a copperhead in the pile of scrap wood. Untidiness offers opportunity: Around fallen trees or junked trucks, the plants move in, the animals follow. Even those tires in the river have their uses; they shelter small fry and act as pseudo-shells for blue crabs during the perilous softness of their molt. Much of the Point's untidiness implies abundance and vigor, the pulsing beat of uncountable lives.

But right here, before I go any further in support of keeping the world in a moderate state of mess, it might be advisable to issue a disclaimer and state quite firmly that I hold no brief for lethal trash— the tossed-aside six-pack rings that strangle seabirds, the batteries that poison landfills with their acids, the million-gallon oil slicks spilled by tankers and tyrants, the industrial wastes bearing heavy metals—mercury, cadmium, lead—that are discharged with the state's permission directly into the river that flows past my front door. The mess I have in mind is earth-friendly junk, the kinds of eyesores that can be recycled in the fashion of the rust-bucket ships sunk by intention off the Carolina coast to provide artificial reefs. There the fish congregate and the fishermen thrive.

Like a sunken ship, like a brushpile, the Point is reef, island, and miniature ecosystem. But it's under assault. The armies have already mustered. The timber companies are clear-cutting the huge pine plantations that once guarded our self-reliant, nineteenth-century way of life with living green walls that kept the onrush of the twentieth century at a respectful distance. The trees are felled, the slash is burned, and the blackened acreage, which can smoulder for days, is sold, because these days it's land, not trees, that puts the money in corporate coffers. The private developers and public agencies have also marshalled their forces for the advance toward our boonies. Phalanxes of yellow bulldozers roar in the vanguard, followed closely by companies of paving machines, cement trucks, and building contractors. On their heels come those who plant territory-claiming flags—the road signs—at every intersection. (How grand and grandiose some of the visions proclaimed by the signs: one half-mile stretch of modest two-lane leading straight to the river is not called road or trail or lane but has, with utter immodesty, been designated a boulevard.) And as the armies bear down closer and closer, the Point begins to forfeit its isolation, which is the font of its independence, its immunity to zoning codes and covenants. What is the future of brushpiles great and small?

It must be admitted that the creeping encroachments of tidiness do bring certain advantages. A year ago, the county's planning office notified all of us living in the rural-mail-route hinterlands that we were to be blessed with street names and an individual number for each habitation. The laudable aim, now an almost achieved reality, is to speed delivery of the emergency services—fire trucks, police, the rescue squad—that used to get lost trying to find us in a maze of dirt roads without names. For those of us who live out here, it's comforting to know that we can indeed be found, and found quickly, when disaster hits.

Along with comfort, however, comes a sense of violation. It is as if we've been tugged closer to town and, worse, made intimately proximate to traffic lights, pizza parlors, and pawn shops. Seclusion, once as dense as a thicket, is being thinned to the vanishing point, and with it goes our anonymity, our wont to do for ourselves.

What will be left of the Point's brushpile? A lot of feistiness, that's for sure. I'd like to see the preservation, too, of at least a residual untidiness. Life thrives in, on, and around clutter. (What else can the Chief and I say, whose garden is one of the weedy kind? But once they've firmly taken root, many vegetables—tomatoes, bell peppers, bush cucumbers, butternut squash, the Blue Lake green beans—seem not to mind the competition.) Clutter provides crevices, and every crevice, from a crack in a fallen log to an old trailer set on a small lot amid the riverside woods, looks like home to somebody.

I'll stick my neck out even farther and wait for the axe to descend: The maintenance of discreet disarray is an act of ecological morality.

Ecological morality—that's the destination, the distant and sweet-singing dream, toward which these stories travel. My two countries, the mountains and the river, give the stories their geographic starting points and also an abundance of birds to contemplate along the way. Focused always on the feathered tribes, the journey also takes place in a temporal dimension that spans at least twenty-five hundred years. Now taking the high road, now taking the low, it often leaves the present moment to go bird-watching on the shores and hills of the past. And with good reason: One of the journey's joyful tasks is to see birds not only as they honestly present themselves in their real and relatively stable natural habitats but also as they've been perceived in the ever-changing, quirky, sometimes untenable habitats of human fancy.

Let me introduce you briefly to some of the people encountered along the way, those who have offered guidance, companionship, entertainment, and occasional misdirection. As in earlier stories, I have consulted natural historians from classical Greece and Rome: Aristotle, the fourth-century B.C. polymath responsible for *The History of Animals*, which is filled with careful and, for the most part, amazingly accurate observations of living creatures; and Pliny the Elder, whose *Natural History*, written in the first century A.D., is an exhaustively credulous, quite wonderful amalgamation of fable and fact. These men stand in the company of ancient poets, particularly two from the far edge of the fifth century B.C.—the tragic playwright Aeschylus and Pindar, who composed high-stepping song-and-dance extravaganzas to celebrate victories in the great athletic games. Both offer instruction in ways of looking at the world; both espouse principles for human behavior amid the welter, the marvels and terrors of everything else. Other poets ancestral in Western

tradition—among them Homer and Virgil—also contribute sometimes sympathetic, sometimes fanciful or wildly apprehensive comments on birds. The old mythographers, named and nameless, are
also here, providing the tales of gods and mortals that are behind the
scientific names with which those of my own day and age have
christened the birds. And this throng of observers is joined by bird-
watchers—people-watchers—from even earlier times, the inspired
Old Testament redactors of Genesis and Job. If their voices sound
somehow bland, unfamiliar, and less than inspired in the quotations
I've used, the reason is that I've chosen the linguistic accuracy of the
New English Bible over the tumbling, sonorous, splendid poetry of
the King James Version. In the former, for example, the Hebrew
word for vulture is translated plainly as *vulture*, not prettified as
eagle.

Nor do my companions in bird-watching come solely from the
long-ago, far-away Mediterranean past. Four of the naturalists from
whom I've sought advice and information are distant not by millennia but by mere centuries. They're closer to home and, hurray, they
speak English.

The eldest among them is one I've consulted before: John Lawson, an Englishman and surveyor general to the British Lords Proprietors of the Carolinas. His book *A New Voyage to Carolina*,
published in 1709, contains an extensive, though far from all-
inclusive, list of the birds to be found along this part of the Atlantic
coast. Lawson has been given credit for being the founder of scientific ornithology in America. But his list, pre-Linnaean and utterly
unscientific in modern terms, is organized by the shrewd but antic
logic of an acute observer into two sections, "Birds" and "Fowls,"
with the former devoted mainly to birds of the land—from raptors to
songbirds—and the latter to birds of the water—swans and ducks,
herons and gulls, and some otherwise unidentified species that Lawson calls Tutcocks and Swaddle-Bills. The list is followed by descriptions, some brief, others packed with page-long detail, of all the
birds mentioned. Many of them were familiar to Lawson because he
had truly observed the very same species at home in England; other
New World birds merely seemed familiar because they bore a close,
but often superficial and therefore misleading, resemblance to the
European birds with which he was well acquainted. Though Law-

son never says so directly, I think it likely that he prepared his list with something other than ornithology in mind. That something was the bird-lusty eighteenth-century palate: Close to one-third of the descriptions contain judgments on whether the species under consideration is good to eat.

Mark Catesby, also an Englishman, is next of the mentors who have given me lessons in ways of seeing the natural world and, in particular, birds found along the mid-Atlantic seaboard. His *Natural History of Carolina, Florida, and the Bahama Islands* appeared piecemeal between 1731 and 1743, whenever he could afford the preparation and coloring of its 220 lavish plates. And of those plates, fully 109 show birds. Catesby accompanied each plate with fairly objective physical descriptions of the avian species and the other kinds of life, mainly plants, that were illustrated. Drawn with vigor and spirit and a bursting, primitive exhilaration, the plates are glorious! Not always lifelike, not entirely accurate, but downright glorious just the same. Catesby's Hummingbird hovers to sip from a trumpet vine's tubular orange flower. In a cutaway view, his American Swallow—the bird we now call the chimney swift—incubates two eggs in the twiggy nest that it has glued to the inside of the favored nest-construction site for which the bird is named. His Blew Jay crouches on the tough stem of a greenbrier vine, its head tilted up, its bill open in a lusty scream. (In typically descriptive, long-winded pre-Linnaean fashion, he designates this jay as *Pica cristata cerulea*—the crested blue magpie.) And his Fieldfare of Carolina—none other than the American robin—lies lifeless, breast to the sky, upon the stump of a snakeroot plant, almost certainly another victim of some salivating eighteenth-century appetite. Catesby didn't always know what he was looking at. One of the two Whipporwills that he delineated snaps its bristle-mustached bill at unlikely food, a leaping mole cricket; the representation is more that of a type than a definite species, for Catesby did not differentiate (nor did he know to do so) between the various well-camouflaged, darkness-loving American members of the Caprimulgidae, or Goatsucker family. Then there's the bird he called the Bastard Baltimore and described as sexually dimorphic, with yellow males and black and "dirty red" females—a bird that he seems to have regarded as either an imposter or a decidedly inferior version of the far more brightly feathered Baltimore bird. He was right about the dimorphism but got the colors backwards. And he was right about the Bastard's close biological connection to the more brilliant Baltimore oriole, but passed on his assessment that the bird was somehow a perversion of the real thing: The eighteenth-century inventor of the binomial system of classification, the man who out-Adamed Adam when it came to putting names on living things—Linnaeus himself—not only picked up Catesby's notion of the bird's illegitimate nature but also picked up Catesby's word and translated it into Latin. Thus, from 1758 to this day, the specific term for the orchard oriole is *spurius*, the bastard. But, though Catesby's knowledge of birds is demonstrably imperfect, it hardly matters. His wide-eyed and inquisitive excitement still sends lively ripples through the present moment.

Just as excited, just as driven by quenchless curiosity, is William Bartram (1739–1823), the third of my guides. The Pennsylvania-born son of a noted botanist, he not only took up his father's profession and became a skilled botanical illustrator but extended his interests beyond the plant kingdom to the entire realm of wildlife. I suspect that being a naturalist gave him the best of all possible excuses to indulge his taste for adventure and succumb most happily to a raging case of wanderlust. He spent four years traipsing through the wilds of the American Southeast. And he made what he calls "ocular observations" of absolutely everything he came across—not just privet and smilax, persimmon and prickly pear, but bees, alligators, rattlesnakes, and a host of birds. One result of Bartram's peregrinations was a book published in 1791, *Travels through North and South Carolina, Georgia, East and West Florida*, which was eagerly read by his fellow Americans and lauded overseas by the likes of Wordsworth and Coleridge. Exuberantly eloquent and filled with a joyful, childlike wonder, Bartram's writing puts any reader, even one coming along two hundred years later, right on the scene. Though anecdotes about birds appear throughout the book, one chapter deals with nothing but their kind and gives the longest list yet of the birds to be found in the eastern United States—215 species. Aware that there were species he'd overlooked, he gave a modest shrug and said that he would "leave them to the investigation of future travelling naturalists of greater ability and industry." As for naturalists of the past, he admired Catesby but took an occasional poke at his predecessor's misapprehensions: "Catesby, in his history of Carolina, speaking of the cat-bird . . . says, 'They have but one note, which resembles the mewing of a cat'; a mistake very injurious to the fame of that bird; he, in reality, being one of our most eminent songsters, little inferior to the philomela or mock-bird." Bartram then goes on to tell how catbirds, imitating what they hear, not only sing sweet melodies but pick up all manner of other sounds, such as the distress cries of baby chicks, which they repeat to the great perturbation of the mother hens. *Omnium-gatherum*—Bartram scooped up everything that came his way, held it out—not always at arm's length—recorded his observations in lovingly abundant detail, and handed them on.

The fourth, and closest in time, of the naturalists who have taken me along on their journeys through American ornithology is a man who needs no introduction—John James Audubon (1785–1851). Suffice it to say that the word-pictures with which he accompanied many of his illustrations serve nearly as well as visual representations to recreate the living birds. In several stories, I have not been able to resist borrowing his artful voice.

The most recent in this throng of guides—all of whom have led me on many a merry chase, sent me off on many a snipe hunt—are some who may not be bird-watchers at all, or not in any conventional sense. They are the poets, among them such keen-eyed observers as Walt Whitman, Robinson Jeffers, Wallace Stevens, and, yes, Edward Lear. The species they study—pelicans, mockingbirds, blackbirds, and all the rest—are birds observed in the mind's eye, birds remembered, imagined, invented, made always larger than life. Nor are the habitats in which they look for birds the usual yards and fields, woods, mountains, and river shores. Instead, the poets claim a limitless, not always mapped territory of headlands and heartlands, in which they find the winged hosts of feelings and ideas.

And with that, the moment comes for a third and final confession.

These stories aren't about birds at all. Or they are, but only in appearance, in the colors of their feathers and, perhaps, their cockiness. Certainly, watching birds for their own sake is an end in itself. Or it's a way of taking wing and leaving earth behind (even for me, who'd rather have a prehensile tail). It's also a means by which we who are not and never shall be birds are able to add new data to the store of scientific facts about the feathered tribes. And possession of more information may help a bit to palliate my species' general ignorance of everything—animal, vegetable, mineral, the whole works—that's not like us. My reasons for observing the avian kind are certainly all of these.

And very likely something more. Can it be, no matter where I exercise my fascination with the feathered tribes, that watching them is one way—and there are many—of contemplating what it is to be alive?

Silence in the Winter Woods

New Year's Day. In these coastal North Carolina woods, it marks a beginning and an ending. On this its first day, the year to come still lies as tightly curled within its frosty, outermost wrappings as an emerging bud. It will swell, unfold, and bloom—that much is sure—but its colors and odors, tastes and textures, are still held secret. But this first day is also the final day hereabouts for one sort of human enterprise: half an hour after sunset, the gun season on white-tailed deer will close.

Except there may not be a sunset tonight, or not one worthy of the name. It is in winter that sunsets blaze over the wide and salty Neuse River in their grandest, most spectacular fashion. December through February, no placid lavenders and pinks, no golden calms illuminate the daylight's last hour, nor does the sun slip gently down behind the far shore five miles away. Instead, it smoulders and glows, bursts into violent flame that spreads like a wildfire igniting every cloud, and when it makes its sudden plunge off the edge of the world, it leaves behind a sky that is still burning, still flaring red-hot along the charred and tattered edges of the clouds. But on this chilly, grey morning of New Year's Day, the auguries for an evening filled with fire and glory do not look promising. An overcast veils the sun, and the air holds a raw, damp smell.

I'm hoping it doesn't rain before I get out of these woods. When that might be, I don't know, nor can I find out, for stillness and silence are the order of the day. I'm at the mercy of the woods and of my friend Betty, who is up a tree. Holding her .243 rifle in hands wearing insulated gloves, she's taken a perch on a tree-stand, a platform attached ten feet off the ground to the trunk of a loblolly pine. I'm directly below, with feet on the ground, butt on the lowest rung of the tree-stand ladder, back against the pine. In one respect, my position is better than hers: Knee-high grass and the delicate bamboo known as Virginia cane protect me from the nippy wind that punches her with hard little gusts. But in another, I'm at a definite disadvantage: She has vistas, she can see over the vegetation that blocks my view. I can see no more than ten feet in any direction from the end of my cold and dripping nose.

She's after deer, of course. Since mid-October, she's spent part of every weekend in the woods, under the trees or up them, but she hasn't yet bagged one buck or doe. She'd certainly like to. It's not that her family's freezer lacks fresh venison; the club to which she belongs shares the meat from each hunt among all the participating members. What she really wants is the huge, happy feeling that her patience and well-honed skills have been duly rewarded. And today's her last chance at a prize until the new season opens next October.

I don't know what I'm after. A revelation? An epiphany? Neither looks likely, not after two slow, increasingly frigid hours of stasis under a tree-stand. When Betty asked me to accompany her on deer season's ultimate day, tagging along with binoculars seemed a fine idea. I'd accompanied her on other such occasions, after all, and had had a great good time looking, listening, being caught up in the hunt's ancient and communal rituals. And this occasion held special promise: The New Year would be greeted not with bleary midnight yawns but with wide-awake zest. I'd be turning in early in order to rise refreshed and eager in the crackling cold darkness just before dawn. Even better, the first day of my year would begin outdoors, with no house walls or any other barrier between me and the natural world. No barrier, that is, except for long johns, corduroys, woolly shirt and woolly hat, and all the other padding needed to keep the January cold at bay. I'm discovering, though, that this bleak reality bears little resemblance to the promise. I'm wide awake all right, but that's about it.

Shortly after 6:00 A.M., when night still held its black sway and the thermometer read forty degrees but a stiff northeast wind brought the real temperature down below freezing, Betty and her husband, Cap'n Harry, fetched me in their white half-ton Ford pickup truck. Fifteen miles and half an hour later, when first light had bleached the blackness to a dingy grey, we arrived at the place selected by the club for its New Year's hunt, a gravel road on the edge of the Croatan National Forest. Their hats and vests blazing orange in the gloom, the hunters rallied with their weapons and deer dogs and pickups. The sun came all the way up as they discussed their plans—who was to take a stand where, when the dogs would be released—but the day did not brighten appreciably. The sky remained as grey as weathered driftwood, nor did the wind abate. The talk and the planning, though, held a contagious vigor, and Betty fairly sparkled with anticipation. She'd spoken right out to choose her spot for the day—the cutdown, as she calls it, in which she'd once taken a mighty fine buck and proved to the club's male members once and for all that, yes, the lady can shoot. And after the day's plans had been laid and everyone had stood around jawing for another fifteen minutes, Cap'n Harry drove us a mile and a half down the gravel road, let us off at the cutdown, and proceeded to the stand he'd chosen. So here we are, she up a tree and I down below on the cold, cold ground. And the day is becoming more shivery, more grey and sullen by the moment. Could be it's fixing to rain before the day is out.

The cutdown doesn't offer a whole lot to do. Nor is it really what I'd consider a cutdown, an area thinned or denuded of trees by the loggers. This place shows no sign of human management or interference. It's more a parkland, an open woods, in which this coast's ever-present loblolly pines, spaced around us in a wide, leisurely fashion, have given themselves plenty of elbowroom, and the understory is not a thicket of briers and vines but a rough carpet of dry yellow grass with a few clumps of equally dry and yellow Virginia cane. And in this place, not even the birds have seen fit to provide entertainment. When we entered it, several brown-headed nuthatches, making a racket with their busy little squeaky-toy voices, were flitting about in the upper stories of the pines. Since then, however, I haven't seen another bird, though I've heard four more species—yelping robin, whooping towhee, caroling wren, and a couple of fussbudget chickadees. But even they have held their tongues for the last hour.

Betty, sitting on her platform, has a gift for maintaining silence and stillness. She does not wiggle or rustle, sniffle or cough. But forty-five frigid minutes ago, she was poised for excitement. And I stopped listening for birds. The distant chorus of the deer dogs rose in pitch: They'd found a scent. The barking and baying got louder, nearer; the pack was running our way. Something started crashing vigorously through the underbrush at the edge of the open woods—oh surely, a big buck! I heard Betty release the safety of her gun. Then all the noise, the barks and the crashes, ceased as abruptly as if someone had flicked a switch. Betty made a soft but definite snort of exasperation. Leaning away from the tree, I craned to look up at her. "Damn puppy," she whispered. "Got lost."

Now the only sounds are the rattles, creaks, and moans created by the northeast wind as it slams its way through grass and pines. The dogs no longer give tongue. The birds do not fly nor call nor hop about. Such inactivity means that they're resting to conserve energy, lying low to avoid exposure to the sharp wind. Or that's the explanation furnished by reason. I know that these woods cannot be so empty as they appear. But, in this near silence, the only sign of creaturely life is my breath rolling white on the cold air. If I lived in an earlier time, I'd know that the birds were sleeping away the harsh weather. I'd know that they'd gone into hibernation.

For most of human history, until a mere two hundred years ago, it was widely believed that many birds did hibernate. Though some hardier species stayed in sight year-round, others of the more tender and delicate sorts vanished in the fall and did not reappear until spring. Where did they go? It was speculated that many of the absent birds, using the bear method, denned themselves in hollow trees or caves for the long winter's sleep. The swallows, however, were said to prefer the turtle strategy; when autumn came, they dived into ponds and lakes, sank to the bottom, and settled themselves in the mud until returning spring bade them wake and rise into its warmth. One marveling rumor had it that some birds did indeed migrate, not hiding from winter's rigors but making a complete escape. Their seasonal destination was not, however, some pleasantly balmy terrestrial spot; instead, they flew over an ocean of space to the gleaming and magical moon.

And in those days, though the Western world assigned great importance to the feathered tribes, they were seldom the focus of objective inquiry. Nor were they admired for their drab or glorious selves. With a few notable exceptions, Aristotle among them, people appreciated birds strictly for their usefulness to humankind. The value of any particular species might be assessed by asking one of two questions: Is it good to eat? What does it advise or predict for the conduct of human affairs?

Eighteenth-century lists of American birds often give answers to the first question; objective descriptions are regularly accompanied by comments on edibility. John Lawson, for example, gave a salivating yes to red-winged blackbirds, meadowlarks, and sandpipers, a disgusted no to pelicans and some, but not all, species of gulls. In the nineteenth century, typical of his day and age, Audubon shot, drew, and devoured many of his specimens, though he never sampled cormorant flesh and vowed not to unless there were nothing better to be had. To this day, wild birds—among them ducks, geese, swans, woodcock, snipe, and doves—are brought proudly home for the supper table. And though a taste for bird flesh may now be legitimately satisfied by licensed hunting or an easy trip to the local supermarket, some people, especially those who were born and brought up in rural backwaters, still regard meadowlarks and robins not as birds but as dinner.

As for the second question, it's flown completely out of fashion. But there were millennia in which sane, reasonable men and women were trained to interpret the songs of birds and their patterns of flight. The songs, of course, were really the voices of gods, and the birds overhead were messengers bearing directions straight from heaven.

Indeed, birds decided the outcome of the contest between Romulus and Remus to see which twin would name and rule the young city on the banks of the river Tiber. So says Ennius, Latin poet of the early second century B.C., who put Rome's history into verse. As he tells it, each brother ascended one of the famous seven hills, Remus choosing an elevation to the east and Romulus one to the west. And there, with kinsmen waiting below, each spent the night in prayer. Remus asked for a single bird, and Romulus asked for many. Then:

> In the dawn's gate, a dazzle
>   an upthrusting light,
> and lured from the pierced height
>   the bird prayed-for plummets,
> its winged shadow raking
>   the sun's rising gold.
> And is joined, tier on tier,
>   by heavenly hosts, a rapture
> of eagles, hurtling home
>   to the sun's risen heart.

So it was that Romulus gained the rights and powers of kinship and its tangible earth. And the city on the Tiber was called not Remora but Roma, the name by which it is known today, some twenty-five hundred years after the eagles made their decisive appearance.

But few people now remember those fateful birds, and certainly no one today would entrust the future course of human events to a bunch of airborne feathers, nor believe that swallows winter in the mud, nor that the white and frozen moon—

Gunshot! Someone maybe half a mile away has fired a rifle. A deer brought down? Betty does not stir. She gives no indication whatsoever that she's ready to leave the tree-stand. So, we'll stay here until she lets me know it's time to walk out to the road. I push the layers of clothing back from my wrist to look at my watch—twenty-six minutes past ten o'clock, nearly two and a half hours of stasis. The meditation on hibernation and augury, the hunt through memory for the lines from Ennius—these removed me from the cold present moment for only twelve minutes. And the temperature seems to have dropped, the sky to have darkened to a grey that definitely predicts a New Year's rain. Damn, but these woods are cold as the moon! Though I try, it's just not possible to return to a reverie that banishes discomfort and monotony by whisking me off to other places, other times, other ways of looking at the world.

But what's worth looking at here in this cutdown? Dark pine-trunk columns that hold up the heavy grey sky and keep it from crashing onto the earth. Walls of winter-killed grass surrounding the small and unkempt courtyard in which I sit. Litter everywhere around my numbing feet. Part of the litter is human trash left by Betty's unknown predecessor up in the tree-stand—hardly weathered cigarette filters and an empty pack wrapped in still-shiny cellophane. And there's a mort of woods trash or duff, as the foresters call it: pine straw, pinecones, broken grass, dry brown leaves blown in from who knows where, deadwood riddled with insect holes, rotten sticks that bear several tiny but surprisingly colorful species of fungus. I wish I knew more about fungus. Quietly, quietly so that the hoped-for end-of-season deer that's sure to be lurking somewhere nearby won't be spooked by an untoward sound, I pick up a short fungus-decorated stick. A dead leaf clings to it, and a piece of pine straw. Oh!

These pines are *not* the usual, tedious loblollies that crowd trunk to trunk in the timber companies' plantations and seed themselves everywhere with the fast-growing, me-first vigor of opportunistic weeds. Loblolly needles are short. But this straw stretches the distance from my elbow to my wrist. And look, cones measuring a full twelve inches lie on the ground not a yard from my boots. Twenty minutes to eleven: It's taken me nearly three blind and shameful hours to see where I am. This open and parklike stand of evergreens is no cutdown, though fire may well have burned through within the last decade. This place in which we've spent the morning of the year's first day is a small and isolated but typical example of a longleaf pine–wire grass savannah. Covering mile on square mile, such savannahs once flourished on this sandy coast. They have immemorially furnished the habitat for several species of birds, notably Bachman's sparrow and the red-cockaded woodpecker, neither of which I have ever seen but would dearly like to. My chances may be slim because, as the stands of longleaf pines have fallen to the axe and to a commercial preference for planting trees—loblollies—that mature more quickly, the birds that require these savannahs for sustenance, shelter, and reproduction have been thwarted. The rusty sparrow has become rare in these parts. The lively little woodpecker, not much bigger than a downy, that excavates its nest cavity in the living wood of a fully mature longleaf pine is now an endangered species throughout its southeastern range. But the pines that surround Betty and me look young, and the several acres on which they stand would not furnish enough land to support a breeding colony of red-cockadeds.

This patch, this remnant of longleaf savannah around us, seems an island amid a sea of dark green sameness, of endless loblollies, an island that even includes a few of these weed trees, one of which I've been leaning against. But a glance shows dozens of long, long cones lying on the ground within my grass-enclosed burrow, and thousands on thousands of long, long needles on the branches overhead. And against the dark grey sky, just above the treetops, flies one of the Buteo hawks, probably a red-tail, though the light is too poor to show anything other than its broad-winged, short-tailed silhouette. If I were a Roman, I would know that its flight is one of the many voices of silence and that the bird shows itself to augur something extraordinary. I would know that it confirms my morning-long occupation of a small yet wholly remarkable kingdom of pines.

Then, from above, there falls to earth an ordinary omen, one of immediate and practical significance: a cigarette ash. Betty is smoking. It means she's called it a morning, she's no longer worried about spooking deer. It means I can stand up and stretch. It means we may break silence. I light up too. Handing me her rifle, she climbs down stiffly from her high, windswept perch. After the hours of stillness, the hours of wind-buffeted quiet, we talk, and though our voices are pitched at perfectly normal levels it seems that we're shouting. She describes the crashing, baying bewilderment of the lost deer-dog puppy. I tell her about the pines, the *longleaf* pines. We both wonder who fired the single shot and if it killed a deer. The sky has become as grey-dark and oily as gunmetal, but it seems almost no time until Cap'n Harry comes along, parks the white pickup on the road beside our woods, and hollers for us to come on out of there, don't make him wait, he's pure-T ready for some food. So are we. He answers the main question about the shot as he takes me back home to the riverbank: a goddamn pitiful miss. He and Betty will return to the field after lunch; no sense letting the last day of deer season get clean away. It will get away, though, for the rain that's threatened all morning will come down drenching and icy cold, driving most of the hunters back to their firesides and their hot-blooded, ten-point dreams.

"Happy New Year," Betty says in her calm, low voice when we reach the river. As I climb the steps to the front porch, Cap'n Harry roars out, "Happy New Year!"

Thank you. Yes.

Dangerous Birds

This story spills the beans about Cap'n Harry and the man I'll call Elgie. It also treats of lust and warfare, of avicide, ornithophagy, and the dilemmas that result from the exercises of such appetites. And it shows me making snap judgments, not to mention exhibiting a shameless lack of charity. First of all, however, it zeros in on birds that are downright dangerous to humankind.

Dangerous *birds?* The answer depends on circumstance and point of view. In the eyes of science, the answer is no—for the most part. 23

But according to myth and the movies, it's yes. And it's yes, selectively, in the nonfictive world of Great Neck Point, where most people manage to escape attack, but those few who are singled out suffer intermittently from sharp, impulsive pecks. Here, though other species are capable of inflicting harm, the birds that strike most often and forcibly are *Turdus migratorius* and *Cyanocitta cristata*, less formally known as the American robin and the blue jay.

Traditional harbinger of spring and flamboyant, fearless scolder of hawks? Clearly some explanation of the threats they pose is called for. Birds are sure culprits when it comes to working certain sorts of indirect harm, mainly to the exchequer. At the Point, we contend with grackles that gleefully harvest newly sprouted seeds, with hummingbirds and orchard orioles that stab and slice open ripening tomatoes with stiletto-like bills. City folks, of course, have long had to cope with pigeons, pigeon droppings, and generally unsuccessful measures to cleanse the urban scene of both. But when it comes to direct damage, no one has ever identified an actual avian equivalent to the shark or the man-eating tiger. Birds do not prey on living people nor inflict malicious wounds. The only injuries a person may sustain from birds are those caused by invading nesting territory or otherwise cozying up a little too close—a raptor's talons sunk deep in an unprotected arm, a clobbering kick from a skittish ostrich. And proximity on a continuing rather than one-time basis is the reason that science lightly qualifies its negative response to the question of dangerousness: People may indeed catch diseases from birds themselves and from their droppings and parasites. Migratory species are, for example, one factor in the spread of Lyme disease; they give long-distance rides to tiny stowaways, the ticks that are the disease's vector. Science, however, looks only at physical hazards. It shrugs off what cannot be seen or quantified.

For another view of bird-borne peril, I consult my friends the Greeks. They tell me that imagination knows full well, and has known for millennia, that danger soars on wide wings and plummets, talons extended, toward earth and human victims. It works its bill like a butcher knife. It croons deadly songs. Some of this knowledge, carried with snug terror in imagination's heart, is based on realistic observation. From watching carrion birds ripping at carcasses, it's easy to extrapolate the vulture that visited divine punish-

ment on the fire-stealing thief Prometheus by tearing out his liver
every day. And some of the knowledge stems from a desire to understand forces that cannot be seen; to endow them with concrete
form is to replace a frightening void with a tangible image over
which mind and heart may feel they have some control. In the
Odyssey, Homer gives us two such images, one that embodies a
physical force and the other, an emotion. Whirlwinds are given the
guise of great rapacious birds, the harpies, whose name means
"snatcher"; they materialize suddenly, fearfully, stooping from aloft
to seize their prey and befoul all that lies in their path. And, as the
harpies make destructive winds visible to the mind's eye, the Sirens
give shape to an aboriginal fear of death at sea. Homer records the
beckoning song of these soft, plump birds with women's heads.
Forgive the poor sailor. Listening to such seductive music, how
could he *not* drown? Sirens and harpies: Because what they represent has not vanished, it may truly be said that these fatal birds exist
to this day.

The Stymphalian birds, thank goodness, do not. Nor is it possible
to tell from what uncomprehending observation, what waking nightmare, they may have been hatched. Among the best sources on their
nature and habits is the gadabout Pausanias, the Fodor of the second century A.D., who toured the shrines and legendary sites of
Greece and wrote a detailed travel guide. One such place was
Stymphalos, a town built near the bog that tradition hallowed as the
site of Herakles's sixth labor. The hero had already slain both the
man-killing Nemean lion and the many-headed Hydra. Without
harming them, he'd captured first a sacred hind with bronze hooves
and golden antlers and then a huge and savage boar. He'd cleaned
the stinking, dung-filled stables of King Augeias by diverting two
rivers through them to carry away the filth. The sixth labor was the
removal of the uncountable birds that roosted in the bog and flew
forth to kill and feast upon the region's helpless populace. The
species, native to Arabia and newly immigrated into Greece, possessed unmistakable field marks: Not only were the birds as large as
cranes or ibis, but their bills, talons, and flight feathers were made
of brass. The feathers could be shot like arrows, and the long, well-
sharpened bill could be wielded like a sword to pierce a human
victim through the heart. And the flock consisted of so many birds

that when it clattered into flight, it blotted out the sun and cast a huge, cold shadow on the earth below. But on the day that Herakles arrived to drive the birds from Stymphalos, they refused to spread their wings and leave the bog. Nor could Herakles approach the cagey creatures, for the moss on the bog's surface covered a deep and mucky soil that would not support the hero's weight. What's a hero to do? Count on a deity to save the day. The goddess Athena, making a cameo appearance, tossed him a brass noisemaker. And Herakles made a sudden, rattle-clacking din that threw the whole flock into panicked flight. With his own arrows, he shot down birds by the hundreds and tens of hundreds. The few that escaped slaughter flew off, never to return. And since that day, there's been no need to fear these brazen predators.

Imagination has, however, granted the concept of avian terrorists a modern incarnation. Alfred Hitchcock's film *The Birds*, based on a story of the same name by Daphne du Maurier, depicts actual rather than mythic species but tries to make them larger than life. Gulls and sparrows and crows gather in enormous, swirling flocks that strike with the force of harpies, with the random, motiveless cruelty of Stymphalian birds. Their brutal beaks, capable of hacking through walls and demolishing houses, are used more quickly and finally to bloody and kill human beings. But in general, the film deals more with poppycock than with real birds; the horror is as artificial as a set of vampire fangs bought at the five-and-dime. If only reasons had been given for the birds' intentional, concerted viciousness, if only the viewer or reader had been allowed to glimpse some latter-day Herakles, the story and the movie might have been redeemed.

Hitchcock may have hoped, however, that his audience would be scared silly by the activation of at least one of two elements. Either element can cause a surge of fear. The first, and lesser, is that the film shows familiar creatures behaving in an unfamiliar manner. "Dive-bombing gull, attack rabbit," says a friend, "that kind of thing can make you right nervous." The second element is ignorance, the ignorance of the young janitor I once saw trying to remove a starling from the lobby of an office. Holding a thirty-gallon plastic garbage bag open like an oversized dark-green net, he leaped and swooped after the frightened intruder. The expression on his face was one of terror, and he might have erupted in a shriek if he hadn't needed to show the other people in the room that he, far bigger than the bird, was in full control of a perilous situation. But he was, after all, dealing with the unknown—a creature of wing-flapping ferocity, with claws that might scratch his face and a long, sharp bill that might peck out his unprotected eyes. Someone else had the presence of mind to open a window so that the starling could fly free. And like the young janitor, someone with little or no knowledge of what constitutes natural behavior (and panic at being trapped and pursued was natural for the starling) may experience tremendous difficulty in separating the ordinary from the strange and threatening. Lack of knowledge makes for a spongelike credulity that sops up every drop of fact and fiction spilled its way. Hitchcock may have hoped to manipulate such credulity and, among other tricks, persuade it that human motives and feelings may be found in birds. Behold: from harpies to man-killing crows and gulls, anything is possible. Birds are dangerous indeed. They become muggers, kamikaze machines, and instruments of capricious but wholly implacable vengeance.

But blue jays and robins? No one in his right mind, not mythographer or moviemaker, would cast these birds in such roles. To begin with, both birds are common—and commonly recognized—species throughout their extensive ranges. Neither spreads plagues of any sort to human beings, nor are they birds of bad repute that ruin fruits and vegetables with greedy pecks or soil the world beneath their perches with overabundant excrement. Evil omens do not shadow them; it is the province of darker birds—owl, crow, and vulture—to bode the coming of death and disaster.

The red, red robin has ever laid claim to North America's affections. It brings good cheer in its happy association with the coming of spring (though various members of the species may indeed be present year-round in a given location). Just as the real bird hops across our lawns cocking its head to look for worms, the lyric bird goes bob-bob-bobbing along through popular song. And the robin has been so admired for its own song that once upon a not-so-distant time, along with cardinals, mockingbirds, and orioles, it was bred in captivity and kept as a cage bird. John James Audubon told of this practice: "The gentle and lively disposition of the Robin when raised in the cage, and the simplicity of his song, of which he is very lavish in confinement, render him a special favorite." And according to Audubon, the pet robin returns its keeper's fondness: "It will follow its owner, and come to his call, peck at his finger, or kiss his mouth, with seeming pleasure."

Blue jays, on the other hand, don't win popularity contests. An informal poll taken in any neighborhood will show that those who despise them far outnumber their partisans. And they do have habits that provoke a certain human squeamishness. In a plate made in 1825, Audubon illustrated three of them in the act of breaking and devouring the contents of other birds' eggs: One jay is shown with an egg impaled on its bill, and another swills the yolk that pours from an egg cracked open by the third. Such a depiction would be coldly accusatory if it were not for the comments that Audubon made to accompany it:

Reader, look at the plate in which are represented three individuals of this beautiful species—rogues though they be, and thieves, as I would call them, were it fit for me to pass judgment on their actions. See how each is enjoying the fruits of his knavery, sucking the egg which he has pilfered from the nest of some innocent dove or harmless partridge! Who could imagine that a form so graceful, arrayed by nature in a garb so resplendent, should harbour so much mischief;—that selfishness, duplicity, and malice should form the moral accompaniments of so much physical perfection! Yet so it is, and how like beings of a much higher order, are these gay deceivers!

Audubon, thank goodness, understood that birds are not to be judged in human terms. He did not, however, hesitate to use these feathered rogues and thieves to take the measure of his own kind.

If blue jays are not viewed through the lens of subjectivity, it is possible to see them, along with the friendly robin, as bright and lively illustrations of the loveliness of ordinary things. Though the jay states its mind with jeers and exclamations, it looks to be a model of suave, unruffled, slightly rakish elegance. Nor is the jay limited to jeers; its repertoire includes extravagant yodels as well as melodic plaints in a minor key. Beside the jay's loud and self-possessed worldliness, the robin seems a pert and wide-eyed child. And how like the sounds of a child are its off-season giggles and titters and yelps. The robin, however, claims his breeding grounds with a full-throated carol.

The worst that can be said of either species is that sometimes, briefly, they may become nuisances. Jays are as quick as mockingbirds to drive other species away from feeders or from any playground they've claimed for a day or perhaps just an hour, and their harsh, nasal calls, endlessly repeated, can shatter a human listener's equanimity and drive him to worse than despair. But jays seem to weary of running off birds that they see as intruders, or else they find less obtrusive ways of using their energies and time. Nightfall and the need to roost can also be counted on to calm and hush them. With robins, the nuisance created is a seasonal phenomenon. On some winter days, they flock so thickly to the Point that one needs an umbrella to walk beneath the trees in which they perch. Umbrella? It's useful as a shield against an incessant, hard-pelting rain of robin droppings.

Blue jays and robins—dangerous to people? Oh yes, but in a fashion quite unlike that of the mythic birds or Hitchcock's make-believe squadrons of crows and gulls. Those monsters not only executed but organized direct attacks on humankind, and they struck with full intent to work most grievous harm. But robins and jays cannot inflict fatal wounds, much less plan to do so. Nor could they truly injure people even if they tried.

"Whoa, wait a minute," says Tommy, red-bearded son of our next-door neighbor. He's taking a river-time break from his high-tech world. "Let me tell you about the blue jays and how my vendetta against them began."

"Vendetta?" I say. "C'mon. That sounds extreme."

He nods. "Vendetta. It started when I was almost eight years old. I was strolling through the yard one day and found this baby blue jay. Bird was screaming its little lungs out. Well, I picked it up, looked up in the tree, and saw the nest. I was gonna do the right thing—climb the tree and put the baby back. But there was pain— sharp *pain.* Something tried to drill a hole in my cranium. Damned if there wasn't a blue jay pecking on my head, and at least five more coming. All of a sudden the air was full of blue jays, and this baby was still in my hand just a-screaming. Only one thing to do—start running. When I got to the porch, I was *bleeding.* Old cat was there watching and waiting to see how things would turn out. Turned out I gave that noisy baby to the cat.

"And about two weeks after that, my daddy asked me what I wanted for my birthday. A BB gun, yeah. It got 183 blue jays the first time around. But you've got to remember—the jays drew first blood. And now I'm thirty-five years old. I have a $500, custom-made German air rifle, and still ain't a blue jay come around *my* property."

Whew! Does the Hitchcock–du Maurier nightmare have substance after all? Not really. Tommy's bleeding cranium in no way demonstrates any viciousness or intentional malice on the part of the jays. Nor does it prove that jays are ipso facto dangerous. Instead, these attack-jays were simply exercising an instinct-bred courage against a much larger enemy who was making off with one of their young. They, like the robins, are basically innocuous and innocent.

It's in that innocence, however, that the danger lurks: The very sight of these birds provokes some people—not many, but a few—to grasp an unfair advantage. The danger posed by robins, jays, and other birds that are equally mild is found in the raging human impulses these species unwittingly excite and in the dilemmas that acting on impulse may create.

It's high time for one of the Point's bird victims to make his appearance. And he makes it with a bang. To be more precise, he makes it with the zinging crack of a .22-caliber rifle.

And Sally Doberman cowers and crawls on her belly into the shelter of an overturned boat. As she's aged, she's become jumpy and timorous about loud, sudden noises—gunshots, firecrackers, sky-splitting claps of thunder. Until the .22 redirected her energies and drove her into quivering retreat, she'd been bouncing along, keeping me company as I walked along the riverfront looking for November birds, particularly the ducks now coming in to spend the winter. My efforts, too, are redirected. It's not a rare occurrence to hear gunshots at the Point, but the sounds usually come from the backwoods, not the nearby river. The waterfront lots are closely built and well populated. Granted, it's Monday afternoon when, in the normal course of events, many residents would be at work, but this particular Monday happens to mark the observance of Veterans Day, a holiday for lots of folks here.

Tz-i-i-i-ng! Who in blue-blazing tarnation is taking potshots in a crowded neighborhood?

Leaving Sal to her boat-shielded trembling, I go to see. Heading in the direction from which the shots have come, I traverse the edge of a small woods, cross a deep drainage ditch bridged by a wide, weathered board, and enter the Point's most bird-seductive yard. It's been landscaped to offer food, water for drinking and bathing, and abundant cover for dodging out of sight. It has food dispensers for every conceivable feeder-visiting species: suet for nuthatches and woodpeckers, thistle seed for goldfinches, nectar for hummingbirds, canned cranberries or fresh oranges for the orioles, and more, more, more, such as peanut hearts and sunflower seeds for wrens, cardinals, titmice, and chickadees. Nest boxes tacked to trees or set on poles are used by flycatchers and bluebirds. And within this unfenced aviary, orchard orioles build basket nests high in the sweet gums, peewees tack little lichen-covered cups to loblolly branches. For two years in a row, a yellow-billed cuckoo has nested in a live oak and, on a rickety-looking platform of sticks, reared five hearty young each time. The yard is a paradise for birds. And in the immemorial manner of paradise, it holds a snake.

Tz-i-i-i-ng! Elgie sits in the open back door of the new, fourteen-by-seventy mobile home that he and his wife pulled into the Eden for birds when he retired and they decided to turn their vacation place into a permanent home. Most of Elgie is concealed inside his trailer. All I can actually see of him are blue-jeaned legs and hands that rest on his knees and point the .22 in the general direction of the feeding-station area and the thickety woods right behind it. Mind's eye, however, gives a more complete audiovisual presentation: Elgie is a short, rotund, bowlegged, pugnacious former military man who attends church with Bible-belt fervor, uses few words, and sometimes does not call his wife by name but whistles loudly when he wishes to summon her. He does not see me. He lifts the gun and takes another shot. It seems a safe bet that he's not shooting at random but rather aiming at feathered targets. Neighbors have reported that Elgie plinks birds as if they were varmints. Seed-snitching grackles, sweet-singing mockers—when his trigger finger feels the itch, it doesn't matter that he fires at birds on which there is no open hunting season. Looks as if I've caught him in the act.

Best to let him know that there's a human being on his shooting range.

I call out, "Any luck?"

"Eh?"

I move closer, sure now that Elgie won't inadvertently aim the .22 in my direction, and repeat the question.

"Damn jays," he says. The yard is indeed a flying circus of jays. Several dozen must be zooming from perch to perch and squawking cuss-calls all the while.

"What's wrong with jays?"

"Drive other birds away." He snorts, as if that point ought to have been self-evident.

But I respond, saying that jays are harmless, not hurting the birds they shoo off, and when the jays weary of such sport, the others always return to the yard. I could have added that these jays of November are left-behind young or recent migrants into the area. Summer's breeding pairs have departed for points farther south. These newcomers are abundantly and raucously proclaiming their intention to winter here.

"Drive 'em away from the feeders, jays do." He speaks slowly, distinctly, making sure I don't misunderstand such a simple problem. He seems convinced that the jays are marauders and usurpers, depriving other species of their rights to food and peaceful coexistence.

Trying a sterner tactic, I tell him that blue jays and other songbirds are protected by law.

He is not swayed. He looks at me as if I were an idiot child, points to his barrel chest, and says "*My* yard."

All right, a man's home is his castle. How, though, can it be made clear to this petty king that, although yard and trailer do indeed constitute his private fief, his property lines do not wall him off from the need to obey state and federal laws. Elgie is free to whistle his wife to his side as if she were a dog, but he is not free to kill her. Nor is he free to slaughter birds—grackles, mockingbirds, and now the jays. But, acting on the reasonable assumption that it is impolitic to mention murder, be it that of birds or a spouse, I take another tack.

"Are the jays hurting you? Is it Christian to kill them?"

"Dominion over fish of the sea, fowl of the air—the Book says so."

Rebuttal from Genesis—well, I asked for that, but not for the shot he uses to emphasize his point. I don't see a jay fall, but I do lose my temper. "Illegal shooting! You're breaking the law! Game warden—"

"Damn jays."

"Game warden could arrest you!" I've gone overboard. I'm shouting.

"*My* yard."

Yes, *his* yard, and I'm standing in it. Though the accusations are legitimate, I'm hurling them from a highly vulnerable position. At this point it matters not a whit that the man's a criminal, an avicidal maniac. The most useful thing I can do is to go, retrieve a trembling Sally, and take us both straight home. I can't, however, resist my own kind of parting shot. "Elgie, lots of houses, lots of people near your yard. Pity if someone got hit."

Sally is not to be found beneath the boat nor in any other nearby hidey-hole. Seething, furious at my intemperate self, yet wishing with all my heart for kamikaze jays—or better, Stymphalian jays to send their arrows straight through Elgie's mean and shameless heart—I trudge on home. Sal's waiting with the Chief in her own safe yard.

Robin red-breast inspires a different but equally fatal lust. And the Point's other victim of birds is downright fond of his nemesis.

"I did. Yes, I did," says Cap'n Harry. "And let me tell you they were damn good, too."

His wife shrugs. "Not me. You'll have to take his word for it."

The Chief and I are agog, for Cap'n Harry has just confessed to eating robins. Not only to eating a mess of them a couple of weeks ago but to shooting them with appetite aforethought. Nor are his words truly a confession, at least not so far as Harry is concerned. No indeed, they're a plainspoken statement of fact. His tone of voice and the expression on his face betray not an iota of guilt or shame. If anything, he takes a somewhat sneaky pleasure in what he's doing.

An uncommon quirk has been revealed in someone we thought we knew reasonably well. Most of our neighbors at Great Neck Point fall into the category of acquaintances. They're people to greet in passing, to chat with over the fence, to work shoulder to shoulder with when high winds hit and high water sweeps over the land. But when the winds die down, the river recedes, and everyday order is reestablished, we go our separate ways. Harry, however, and his wife Betty have become more than this kind of excellent neighbor: They're friends. Betty and I share recipes and secrets. And it's Betty the hunter who has taken me along on the chase, who has laughed at my fall-in clumsiness at crossing water-filled ditches and, at the same time, given me a glimpse of Artemis hunting deer with her hounds in the North Carolina piney woods. Harry drops by in his white Ford pickup almost nightly after work, announcing his presence with a loud, high-pitched "Whooo!" He and the Chief share companionable silences as they sit in our cedar swing on hot summer nights. At any time of year, they share hoary jokes and giggle like a couple of overgrown kids.

I don't know what we'd do without Harry. The Chief's vegetable garden flourishes because Harry brings over his tiller and breaks the ground before March is out. Thus, the Chief can plant by mid-April, way before summer heat sets in. Harry brings his tiller back to keep the rows weed-free until peppers and cukes, tomatoes and beans can hold their own against witchgrass, bindweed, pigweed, and dock. Not only does he help us reap a bountiful crop from the land, he's also the purveyor of the Chief's favorite crustacean, the succulent shrimp. Some of the shrimp, not many but enough for an evening's entertainment, he catches himself in the river. His sixteen-foot fiberglass workboat, with a powerful 85-horse Evinrude motor, can be rigged with a shrimp trawl, a net fashioned into a long bag that's kept open by a heavy wooden trawl door, or otter board, and pulled slowly behind the boat. After forty-five minutes or so, the net is hauled in and its contents dumped into a waist-high culling box, in which brown shrimp are sorted from blue crabs, two-inch baby flounder and croaker, barnacled shells, and plain old beer-can, pop-bottle trash. One Sunday night several Julys ago, while I was aboard, the shrimp were mainly elsewhere, and two pulls produced a scant seven pounds, enough for two middling greedy appetites at most. But effort and boat fuel were hardly wasted, for Harry had spent the evening at his all-time favorite pursuit—messing around on the water in a boat, aside from which he'd filled two five-gallon buckets with softshell crabs. Harry's workaday job keeps him indoors at a desk, but if there can be such a thing as a full-time avocation, his is to deal in seafood. And when he really wants a load of shrimp to sell, he goes to the coast and, particularly, to the fish houses at which the commercial shrimpers disgorge their catches. Then he proceeds to supply shrimp to salivating customers from this coastal area all the way inland to Raleigh. The Chief and I buy fifty pounds at a crack from him—and spend the rest of the morning heading and packaging the sweet little critters. Accustomed now to eating shrimp that are only hours removed from their native waters, we can no longer stomach the aged, fishy-tasting offerings in the markets.

Harry and the coast and his consumption of robins are inextricably connected. To begin with, not just anyone can go to the area that's known in this part of the world as Down East and come away with several hundred pounds of fresh-off-the-trawler shrimp at a rock-bottom price. Many people, I among them, can't go there and pick up any amount of shrimp at any price, no matter how hard and often we try. Down East is the land that stretches eastward along the mainland side of Core Sound from Beaufort to Cedar Island, from which point a ferry plies across Pamlico Sound to Okracoke on the Outer Banks. Down East is also more, much more, than marshes and coastal woods and quiet, water-laved communities that have long depended on the sea for a living (though tourists and development make inroads now). Down East is most truly a collective state of mind, call it tribal, that honors tradition and is fierce to protect its own. To my outsider's eyes, it seems that protection extends to ignoring us foreigners politely but so adamantly that family and friends make not only the best deals but every single deal that can be made. I've seen the fish-house men look sideways at Betty—until she has identified herself as the wife of Cap'n Harry Ward. Then she gets smiles, action, and half a dozen fifty-pound boxes of fresh-caught, iced-down shrimp piled into the back of her Bronco. Harry, of course, is Cedar Island born and bred.

The title Cap'n is an honorific, having to do partly with Harry's inclination to mess with boats and seafood and partly with the fact that he'd make a living in the fashion of his ancestors if only pound nets and gill nets and trawling could provide his family with more than a hand-to-mouth living. A good many of his kinfolks still live on Cedar Island, where Harry was born in the early 1940s, when leaving the island meant boarding a boat. No bridge had yet been built to span the salt marshes and join the maritime outpost to the mainland. Like many other Cedar Islanders, Harry's daddy made his living as a commercial fisherman, work he left later, when Harry was in his teens, to become a Methodist preacher. Pulling in fish, pulling in souls—both are vocations that net satisfaction but very little cash.

"So," Harry says, "we took care of ourselves. Wasn't any supermarket around the corner either. We lived on fish, ate the vegetables we grew in our garden, hunted wild birds for a little variety. Not just robins either, but meadowlarks. Now there's a stupid bird. Meadowlarks have the ability to fly a great distance, but they don't. They fly and set down only fifty yards away. Makes 'em easy to hunt. We also ate flockbirds. That's what we called 'em—flockbirds. They're really cedar waxwings, fly around in a flock, perch by the flock in their favorite trees—holly, cedar, myrkle bush. You'd call it myrtle. One shotgun shell would kill twenty, thirty flockbirds. You need a bunch to make a meal."

I'm reminded of Audubon's tale of the basketful of cedar waxwings, a delicacy much esteemed in those days, which was dispatched via riverboat as a Christmas present to someone down in New Orleans. The birds never arrived, and it was later discovered that the boat's steward had cooked these little treats and served them up to the passengers. A hundred years later, under the circumstances of Harry's isolated, self-sufficient growing-up, I can understand the eating of songbirds, and I tell him so. "But Harry, that was then, and this is now. This close to the twenty-first century, how can you possibly justify robins?"

For a preacher's son, Harry has a mighty irreverent tongue. "I don't justify 'em, goddammit, I stew 'em."

Feeling that we've been granted a rare and peculiar peek at arcane tribal practices, we listen as he provides his recipe. "Pluck and clean 'em good to start with. Save the legs and breasts and put 'em in a pot. Cover with water, add salt and pepper and a piece of fat meat. Then you cook 'em a long time over low heat till they're nice and tender and also done."

Betty shakes her head but smiles. "Ate 'em all up, he did."

"All but the bones," Harry says in a no-nonsense tone of voice.

"Harry," I protest, "you ought to know better."

"*De*-licious." Totally unrepentant, Harry smacks his lips. Then he looks at me. "Come now, you're adventurous. Like to try some the next time around?"

Robins may also be dangerous to me. I find that I'm tempted.

On the surface it might seem that avicide and ornithophagy—the murder of birds and the eating of same—should present no questions or dilemmas. Clearly, Elgie and Cap'n Harry have broken both state and federal laws by killing what are classified as "protected nongame species." (So has Tommy, but forgiveness goes readily to the bloodied eight-year-old who fed the cause of his torment to the cat. The grown man, however, plays in a far less innocent league.)

Throughout the country, state laws tend to be modeled on the federal statutes restricting the extent to which people may interfere with birds—no collecting of nests, eggs, or feathers, no killing of migratory species. And because birds pay no attention whatsoever to state lines, just about every species is considered migratory. In North Carolina, the classification "protected" covers every native species for which a hunting season has not been sanctioned, with three exceptions. In season and with clearly spelled-out limits, North Carolina's licensed gunners may legitimately take most kinds of waterfowl and also such birds of fields and woods as turkeys and grouse, bobwhite quail, mourning doves, woodcock, and even the common but clever crow. Sometimes, in the face of a perilously dwindling population, a species of game bird will be declared off limits to hunters and its season closed until further notice; one good example is that of the canvasback duck. But from gloriously accomplished songsters such as mockingbirds and cardinals to silent species such as pelicans and vultures, from bold, high-flying hawks and eagles to the reclusive thrushes and wood warblers, nearly all other birds are forbidden quarry. Even obvious pests are protected—the blue and screaming attack jays, the cowbirds that parasitize the nests of other species, and the crop-destroying grackles (these and other blackbirds may create such great losses that the state's guardians of wildlife will permit human retaliation, though only after the damage has been done). The trio of birds that are considered fair game at any time of year consists of species on which the state has slapped the label "nuisance": starlings, house sparrows, and rock doves. The last term is a euphemism for plain old pigeons. Not one of this trio frequents Great Neck Point.

As for robins and blue jays, Elgie and Harry have flouted the law. Clearly then, those who enforce the law ought to be summoned to stop and punish their illegal acts. Or should they?

A better question is, can enforcement be summoned? Can it even be found? The state has entrusted the protection of birds to the Wildlife Commission, and the cops to call are the Commission's game wardens, or wildlife officers as they're formally known here. It's one thing, however, to know in general whom to summon and quite another to learn the local warden's name and telephone number. The number of the Commission itself is not listed in our local directory, nor does it appear in many of the directories that serve small towns and rural areas. The latter are, of course, the very jurisdictions in which the game laws are most likely to be violated because they, not cities, provide wild living spaces for wild critters, the deer, black bears, and alligators, as well as the birds. Contacting the Commission requires, first, a call to information for the number of its headquarters in Raleigh, the state capital, and second, a long-distance call at the caller's expense to find out just who is in charge of policing a specific area down in the boondocks. I decide to spend two bits to telephone Raleigh and obtain the name of the warden whose territory includes Great Neck Point.

It's harder by far to learn something about the value placed by law on a robin, a blue jay, or any other protected, migratory bird. I never do come up with definite figures; in fact, there may be no such figures in the state of North Carolina. But two people who spend their working hours with wildlife offer two educated opinions. A game warden tells me that the usual penalty would amount to a grand total of sixty-two dollars, with court costs accounting for fifty-two dollars of that sum. Thus, in his opinion, a protected bird is worth a sawbuck. Make that birds—plural. The warden says that at the court's discretion the ten-dollar fine may be assessed not by the bird but by the incident. My second informant shakes her head and says the situation's far more grim. She is the executive director of the Outer Banks Wildlife Shelter, where broken birds and animals are mended, if possible, and people are given a glad chance to meet and learn about other forms of life. She says (and the Wildlife Commission later confirms) that the state uses an arcane formula developed by the Commission's biologists to determine the value of a bird and that the formula is meant to calculate what it would cost the state to capture a particular kind of bird and bring it into the state to replace the one lost. The cost varies according to the rarity or commonness of the species. A quiet but still angry despair invests her voice: Once, not long ago, she took the side of a bird in court, a sharp-shinned hawk that had been stoned and grievously hurt by workmen in the industrial building it had chosen as its home. But the men were only obeying orders from the boss, who'd told them to clean up the place. According to the formula, this small, fierce, and beautiful but not uncommon accipiter weighed in at something under three dollars. In monetary terms, even with court costs added in, it takes very little to measure a bird. Thus, robins are doomed to the stewpot, blue jays to plinking, and hawks, of course, shall be tormented in the name of following orders—unless a judge should happen to be an ardent friend to avian life.

That is, if a killer of birds were brought to court in the first place. A biologist with the U.S. Forest Service tells me, "Federal and state, all of us in the field will bust our butts to save wildlife. But somebody shooting birds—around here I doubt you'd get law enforcement to take it to court. They won't take it because the judges are not educated in wildlife law. The judges would also weigh it against human crime—theft, murder, a crowded docket. Against that, it does not seem important."

My problems do not arise, however, in the trouble it takes to find out who's in charge of local enforcement, nor in the blue-moon possibility that a case would ever get to court, nor in a fine set so ludicrously low that it cannot protect any jay or robin from an itchy trigger finger or itchy taste buds. The thought of having to pay a four-star restaurant price—those court costs—for an ill-gotten dinner will not faze Harry when his hunger for little birds turns into a harpy, snatching him up in its avid claws and whirling his appetite out of control. Nor is there any statute that prohibits him from cooking and eating songbirds once they are gunned down with number-nine birdshot. As for Elgie, having to ante up a fine for something he almost certainly regards as fair and just sport—well, that could get him plumb riled.

And the possibility of stirring up that kind of trouble is part of one dilemma. Living in rural isolation is a circumstance that mandates neighborliness. Even in this new day of named streets and numbered houses throughout the county, this long-awaited day of 911 emergency services, it still may take an hour or more for rescue squad or police to arrive at the Point—an hour or more, that is, until trained professionals can begin to work their saving measures. And until they come, we are obliged to count on one another for help. Although no rule decrees that we must like our neighbors—indeed, some may qualify as lunatics or monsters—it's in our mutual interests to work for peaceable coexistence. Making on-the-spot enemies or bearing a hard grudge does not bolster anyone's chances for gaining assistance and assuring safety or, in the worst event, survival itself.

So far as I know, Elgie is harmless, though sometimes rude, in his dealings with other people. And, to give credit where credit's due, he's also rendered occasional help, mainly in retrieving the lumber from storm-broken piers and reuniting it with its rightful owners. It's Elgie's disregard for other forms of life—his almost willful wearing of blinkers—that makes it difficult for me to approach him, much less to trust him. But I have a choice: Stay in the frying pan or leap straight into the sizzling flames. That is, in an attempt to spare the lives of mockingbirds and jays, shall I summon the game warden? Or, to maintain some delicate equilibrium in the human community, must small, bright, noisy lives be forfeited? Shall I stand by looking at a wrongful act but doing nothing to prevent its likely recurrence? In a case like this, the warden is an essentially impotent figure, but he might be persuaded to make stern, authoritative citation of the appropriate statutes and put some fear of the law into Elgie's future behavior. Trouble is, Elgie would quickly realize that he can get away with unsporting, scofflaw tactics so long as I'm not around. For me to try to change his ways would be as futile as his own war against the jays, an effort that seems predicated on teaching those damn birds that his yard is lethally unsafe. If only the jays were capable of a no-holds-barred Hitchcockian assault! In this instance, the real birds, unlike their cinematic counterparts, would have a solid motive for the strike.

Obligations to the human community versus respect and active support for nonhuman forms of life—this real and necessary debate covers a territory far larger and far less parochial than Great Neck Point. And with the big issues in mind, what do I do? Nothing. Oh, I grumble to friends and acquaintances about the Point's avicidal maniac; I even make a wishful murmur to Elgie's wife that he would stop shooting protected birds. But I do not alert the warden and may never do so. Nor am I at peace with my own inanition. But that is a dull ache compared to the most painful consequence of catching Elgie at his lordly game: Because of my runaway tongue, I've forfeited much pleasure. Elgie's yard is not off limits, but when I sneak across its boundary lines, after having made sure that Elgie's not in sight, I feel like a trespasser. Where are the answers?

The dilemma foisted on me by Cap'n Harry is not like that presented by Elgie, though the cases of both men are identical in two respects: Each stands foursquare and stubborn on the wrong side of the law, and neither is a one-shot malefactor but repeats his offense over and again. One difference, however, is that Harry knows full well he breaks the law, though he feels no guilt or compunctions. Certain factors do mitigate his crime. One is that the culture and customs to which he was born have not only permitted but smiled upon ornithophagy. And it's a safe bet that some of today's Down Easters indulge at will in such gourmandizing. A Down East cookbook, published in 1987 by women of the Harkers Island United Methodist Church, includes recipes for fried robins and robins stewed with rice. The recipes are prefaced with the warning that they "call for game that is presently illegal to hunt and kill" and that their inclusion in the book represents a bow to tradition and is "not meant, in any way, to encourage illegal activity." To someone who's addicted to the taste of wild birds, this warning is probably as useful as the surgeon general's warning on a cigarette pack is to a hardcore smoker. And I'm told that even in these modern times some Down Easters, not all of them from an elder generation, say, "If it flies, it dies." The unspoken corollary is that birds were put on this earth for people to eat—and not just the sweet singers but also such birds as cormorants and loons. But they do eat what they kill. And in Cap'n Harry's case, the second mitigating factor is that, like his kin, he uses what he shoots. Elgie simply lets the dead jays fall where they will, nor does he give what Cap'n Harry would call a rat's ass. But Harry does not waste his kill. He does not shoot for sport or for revenge but to acquire food, which he cooks and consumes, "all but the bones." Granted, he can buy perfectly legal bird meat; in season, he can hunt and bring home ducks, quail, woodcock, and snipe. And there's the rub. To what extent does adherence to tradition, to the way he was raised up, really exculpate a malefactor? Or the fact that he makes hearty use of the proceeds of crime? Then, because it's obvious that the Chief and I are fond of Harry, a more basic question may be, does friendship allow the overlooking of a definite, if minor, misdeed? What's more important anyhow, a person or a bird?

People or birds—now that may be the most basic question of all.

"I have two things to say about the snail darter," says Cap'n Harry.

Snail darter? How do we get from dangerous birds to an endangered fish? It happens this way.

On the balmiest of mid-April evenings, Harry and his wife and the Chief and I sit outside keeping river watch. The spring's first bumper hatch of big, hungry bloodhawk mosquitoes whines around our ears and descends on our bare flesh, but the aggravation can be tolerated, ignored even, because we've been granted only a handful of outside evenings so far this year. Newly blossomed honeysuckle sweetens the air; bird song rings loud and melodious in the hedgerows; striped mullet, unusually whopping for this time of year, jump from the water and splash back. Indicators like the size and number of spring mullet already predict a good—perhaps a great—year for catching fish. The sun plunges into the river and tints it rose-gold. The air blows fragrant. The fish still jump, but the sun's disappearance hushes the birds—except for the robins. In the luminous half hour after sundown, until true dark arrives, it is their springtime wont to keep on trilling their treetop serenades.

The red-breasted singers are safe now from Harry's number-nine birdshot. The reason is that he declares a moratorium on the taking of such nongame species during the nesting season. By all means, let robins propagate and create ever more of their kind. And, by some wondrously fortunate ignorance of avian biology, Harry reads the duration of the nesting season as lasting for a long eight months, from the mid-March bloom of pussy-willow catkins to the falling of November's last withered sweet-gum leaf. Or, to put it in terms that better reflect Harry's maritime heritage and interests, from the time the crab pots go into the river to the time they're taken out. This evening the robins, tunefully unaware of their great good luck, enjoy Cap'n Harry's benign inattention. I'm not sure that he even notices their rollicking song. Nor, on such a fine, friendly evening, does it seem appropriate to bring up the subject of robins; mention of the bird might lead to snide remarks on my part about their slaughter and ingestion. I've vowed not to eat them, no matter how tempted.

But a matter for pondering comes silently to mind: What would the Point be like if lots of people developed a ravening fancy for the flesh of robins and other wild songbirds? A taste for little birds is one major factor in the severe decline in the populations of many songbird species overseas, including the skylark celebrated by Shelley, Keats's nightingale, and the European robin with orange breast and russet back. Centuries ago, it was the Dutch who invented the bird feeder as an aid to trapping supper meat. Nowadays, modern laws protect these birds throughout Europe, but no matter—they are ruled fair game by ancient habit and by an equally ancient sense that other creatures were put on earth to serve humankind. And a common assumption is likely at work: Fish in the sea, birds in the air, with so many of *them*, how can *we* do them in? And if something benefits us, how can we possibly harm it? Result: At this late stage of the twentieth century, in Italy alone, fifty million illegally taken robins, larks, and other songbirds wind up on the dinner table each year. Fifty million! But even that boggling number does not begin to approach the full number of European birds in trouble because they're being crowded out by the alteration and outright destruction of habitat as their territory is claimed for human uses, and because they're being killed by the chemicals used in farming and industry.

Though Americans, outside of a few aberrant souls like Harry and his fellow Down Easters, don't eat wild birds, we certainly do subject them to other powerful pressures. In general, more people mean fewer birds. Suppose that Cap'n Harry is merely the tip of a huge appetite and we run out of robins. Suppose, as well, that blue jays come to stir such widespread and trigger-happy ire that we run out of them, too. Would we miss these common species? How would their vanishing affect the world? Did the death of the ultimate passenger pigeon somehow alter the fates of all other living things, including humankind?

Splash, splash, splash—a mullet makes its skipping-stone jump. I ask my questions this way: "Hey everybody, what do you suppose might happen to people and other critters if all the world's mullet were wiped out?"

"Nothing," says the Chief. "Flat-out nothing, except that mullet lovers like you would have to go just a little bit hungry."

From there, the talk leaps easily from abundant, taken-for-granted species to those that are rare, threatened, endangered. Who cares anyway about creatures like mullet, creatures that are so plentiful and ubiquitous that they're almost like trash? The snail darter swims naturally to the surface of conversation because it provides a primal illustration of the conflict that arises when the existence of a small, scarce critter puts a large crimp into man-made plans.

"Two things to say about the snail darter," says Cap'n Harry pontifically, "and one is, who gives a shit? Should a minnow so small you can hardly see it keep a dam from being built? Seems to me that economic interests should come first. The second thing is, that pipsqueak fish may be tougher than you think, able to hide itself away, then show up thumbing its nose. Could be it's like a little version of—what's that fish they caught off the coast of Africa?"

"Coelacanth," says his wife.

"A little version of that, thank you. Now everybody thought that monster was extinct. Fooled us, didn't it. Frankly, my dear, I'm for dams, not some puny, two-bit fish."

We speak then of other animals that have more recently given rise to furors large and small: North Carolina's red-cockaded woodpecker that's forced the scaling back of a road-building project so that a tract of the dwindling longleaf pine savannah in which it nests may be preserved; the Northern spotted owl that has caused hotly contested cutbacks in old-growth-forest logging operations in several states of the Pacific Northwest; the Mt. Graham red squirrel, a subspecies that's halted the construction, atop the eponymous mount, of a telescope capable of peering into the far reaches of space. Endangered species like these tend to polarize human responses—support for the critters at all costs versus gung-ho promotion of man-designed projects, with scarcely a passing thought for the critters.

"Goddammit," says Harry, "our economic interests ought to come first."

"Whoa back. Not necessarily," I reply. One of the virtues of friendship is that friends may disagree, yet remain on not just civil but excellent terms. Harry's view of the way things ought to be is found as commonly as mullet in the river and robins in the hedgerows. And its commonness means that it cannot be overlooked but must somehow be dealt with.

Betty comes to my aid and says in her calm, firm voice, "Harry, we don't always know where our best interests lie. I'll tell you one thing that could vanish, though, and nobody would miss it—these blasted mosquitoes."

"Getting to you, are they? Let's take you home."

The debate shall resume on another, not-so-distant evening. It will never, of course, settle the questions. No one in the world now knows, or shall ever know, enough about the interconnectedness of all life to answer the questions conclusively. But the conversations offer one forum for exploring possibilities and for shaping a viable response to every living thing that is not human. I think that the aim is to achieve some balance, some sapient equilibrium amid a protean swirl of animals and plants—not an easy feat of acrobatics, for it involves standing on a teetering board and juggling at least three slippery balls: aesthetics, ethics, and utility. To pull off such a stunt may well demand some drastic redefinitions of beauty, honor, and long-term practicality.

If the plug is pulled on mullet or robins and blue jays, if they or any other present-day form of life go down the drain along with the long-lost trilobite and tyrannosaurus rex and the not-so-long-lost Carolina parakeet and dusky seaside sparrow, what happens to people? In the eons since life on earth began, ninety-nine percent of all species ever extant have either become extinct or, to a lesser degree, undergone such metamorphic evolutionary redesign that they have been transformed into other species altogether. Thus, at one time of another, most of the strands in the life web have been snapped without destroying the entire fabric. Like a five-lined skink growing a new tail, the highly mutable stuff seems able for the most part to repair itself. So, what are *T. migratorius* and *C. cristata* worth to us, apart from a piddling few dollars, plus court costs? It might be nothing. It could be everything. We just don't know.

We don't know, and maybe we can't know. How many are fifty million? How long is an eon? A lot of people, including me, are simply not able to invest such enormous ideas with sensible everyday meaning. The issues are greater than we are, and far longer lived. Nor are they easily reduced—put, that is, into terms small enough so that a brain not much bigger than a grapefruit can understand the uncountable millennia and the vast forces behind nature's slow work. The very smallness of the here today, gone tomorrow human mind may well be the largest problem faced by anyone who'd promote an agenda for conservation and respect for other life. How difficult it is to push Jane Doe and Joe Blow, Cap'n Harry, Elgie, and me toward altruism or blind faith and to persuade us that our present actions will—yes, they certainly will—have some definite, though not predictable, effects in maybe six or seven generations. We won't be around to see what happens though, or collect any prizes for being the good guys. The only certainty in the scenario is that consequences follow actions and events. That's all we can know. And so long as we know nothing else, then robins and blue jays are dangerous, along with all the other lives we take for granted. And we, the only animals capable of self-annihilation, are a threatened species.

People or birds? Which are more important?

Wait a minute! The proposition is not one that demands an *or*— one *or* another. It needs an *and*—one *and* another, one *and all* of the creeping, swimming, running, flying, and green-growing things. Balance, equilibrium, a meeting in the middle—but until that happens, beware.

Beware of robins and jays, mullet, shrimp, blue crabs, and even mosquitoes. Beware of honeysuckle, pussy willows, and sweet gum trees. First and foremost, beware of self.

*   *   *

Elgie's wife telephones just after lunch to say that veeries—three of them, not a bit shy—have been hopping about on the grass in her front yard all morning long. Did I see them when I made my early walk? "No? Well, come on over, then, They're still here."

It's the first week in September, skies blue, the air still summer-hot and steamy, but the birds know that daylight hours are on the wane and shivering nights lurk just around the corner. They're heading south. Great Neck Point offers a fine selection of places to spend a day or a week en route—the hedgerows, the gardens being put to bed, and several brushpiles, including one the size of a small yacht in our neighbor Lana's field. And one of the migrants' most favored stops is Elgie's yard, with its excellent cover, bathing facilities, and restaurants. Not only are the many feeders stocked with a variety of store-bought goodies, but there's a gourmet menu of wild food from bugs to berries, especially the purple berries that cluster on the black tupelo tree, or black gum as it's called here. Every September, I gawk at that tree in Elgie's front yard till my neck gets kinks from looking upward and my arms begin to quiver a little from trying to hold the binoculars steady. The black gum is a main attraction for several species that rarely visit the Point except in the rolling, frenzied weeks of the autumn migration. Here rose-breasted grosbeaks pause, and scarlet tanagers, northern orioles, western kingbirds, veeries.

As I walk toward Elgie's, Sal keeps me company, trotting ahead, falling back to inspect the underbrush or sniff at some informative scent. She has, of course, completely forgotten that gunshots from that yard once scared the daylights out of her. I still feel like a trespasser, though, every time I walk along its edges. But today an invitation has been issued.

The veeries are there indeed, small brown-backed thrushes with creamy, lightly freckled breasts. Elgie's wife points them out as they hunt for food through the green, oak-shaded grass. Wonderful! A species not just for the month's list of birds but for the year's! And something even more wonderful happens.

"You know why he was shooting those birds?" she says. "To please me! I complained about how jays and mockers chase the other birds away. So he thought he'd do me a great big favor by getting rid of them. Don't you worry now. All it takes is me not telling him when some bird makes me mad. He won't do it again, and that I can guarantee."

I've been too quick to judge the man. Bird plinking sprang from a wish to please the woman he whistles at. Though his actions were lawless, his motives were not. And it's somehow clear that his whistling doesn't bother her a bit. I'm ashamed of myself.

It's also clear that there's no one method of encouraging lawful behavior. I wonder what might be done to reconstruct Cap'n Harry, who is—except for eating little birds—a generally fine and upright man. Most likely, there's nothing that will change his habits. I foresee, however, that his sons will abandon ancestral ways, partly because necessity does not dictate eating wild food unless it's legally hunted deer and ducks, and partly because their wives will flat-out refuse to consider cooking such things as robins and flockbirds. It may also come to pass that our children and their children will have an awareness greater than their parents' that the world of living things is a jackstraw heap—pull out one element, and the others assume new configurations or tumble down. But Elgie—oh joy and jubilation!—has glimpsed the light, though he was converted through his uxorious feelings, not by any reasoned appeal to his better instincts.

"Thank you, thank you!" I tell his good wife. I'd like to whoop with glee, but restraint seems the better tactic—a loud, sudden holler might frighten the veeries. We watch the birds for a few more minutes till Sal, taking off after a rabbit, sends them flying for cover.

And on the way home, my black and rust companion bounding fearlessly along, I think that there's hope after all for us dangerous birds.

What the Wren Says

Teakettle? Chirpity?
Cheery? Wheedle?

That's what the field guides tell us to listen for. That's how they
render the song of the Carolina wren, and they're partly right. Often
as not, the plump little bird utters three loud and nigh dactylic
syllables or sings out a trochee doubled and redoubled. But my ear
has never heard, not even once, any version of wren song found in
the standard field guides. There was a time, though, that I would

49

have sworn by *trickier, beefeater,* and *peashooter,* with occasional nonsense like *petersill* thrown in. And I'd have transcribed the doublets as *tricky* or *cheaper* or *me-too.*

Except that sometimes the Carolina wren makes its song out of only one reiterated syllable—*cheer-cheer-cheer.*

Except that no wren sings in English, or in any other language known to humankind. And sometimes they do not sing at all but utter a series of scolding notes, dry as old leaves shaking in a brisk wind.

Four members of the wren family, the Troglodytidae, are found at Great Neck Point on the lower Neuse. *Troglodytes,* the Den-Diver—that's the word used by Aristotle to describe any animal, such as fox or snake, that would bolt with all haste into the nearest den or other hidey-hole when something disturbed it. Not long after Aristotle, the word slid easily onto the bumptious little wren found then and now in Europe. How exactly it describes the vanishing act performed by this one bird and also its family's habit of ducking for cover, of dashing quickly at the slightest alarm—or no alarm at all—into deepest underbrush or darkest crevice. Three of the Point's four Den-Divers are transient, but one, the loudest and largest, stays most stubbornly put. That one, of course, is the Reed-Leaper from Louisiana, *Thryothorus ludovicianus,* better known as the Carolina wren. And year-round, in January as well as June, it favors rendering its song in a ringing, full-throated, fortissimo holler. Nor is it as shy as the trio of come-and-go wrens.

Each of these three most vividly illustrates the family's penchant for concealment, or rather for keeping their bodies safely out of sight but at the same time loudly advertising their general whereabouts with some sort of vocal hullaballoo. Two of the three arrive to take up hibernal residence when the hedgerows put on autumn colors—when smilax wears loose strands of night-blue berries, and privet, tight clusters of olive green; when sumac and Virginia creeper are decked in scarlet and the sweet gums in pale gold; when plump persimmons glow like orange coals. One of the Point's cold-weather wrens bears a name twice as big as its tiny brown self—den-diving Den-Diver, *Troglodytes troglodytes,* the winter wren. It's the very bird that Aristotle would have seen, indeed the only species of wren that's known in Europe. Its Dutch name translates as "winter king," and one of its British nicknames, cutty quean, means "bobtailed hussy." That's an apt name for this bird that bustles, cocking its stubby tail and brazenly scolding the rest of the world. And it sings, oh it sings; even in winter, when few birds make music, not only its scold but its soft, high, altogether agile coloratura may be heard. The other winter resident is the den-diving nightingale, *T. aedon*, another plain brown bird, capable of singing as sweetly as its namesake or, like all wrens, raising a great and imperious fuss. Though it behaves like an autocrat, its understated appearance is matched by its thoroughly domestic common name, the house wren. The third of the come-and-go wrens—the Rockrose-Leaper of the swampy places. *Cistothorus palustris*—may be heard, and sometimes seen, at any time of year. (The bird does leap, but why the taxonomist has it leaping on a *cistos*, or rockrose, it's hard to say, for many of the woody herbs so designated are found only in poor, sandy soils. But the swamp mentioned in the bird's species name is entirely appropriate.) This is the marsh wren that may be found in any season at the Point. Lurking in the cordgrass and needlerush that fringe the pond, it gives away its general whereabouts by scolding with a hard, reiterated chip-chip-chip or uttering softly, over and over, its untuned, rinky-tink, toy-piano song. But if the marsh wren is one of the come-and-go species, how can it be present year-round? Because the pairs that breed here in the clement spring depart for points south when autumn comes; they are replaced by birds that spent their summer in regions to our north.

Unlike these somewhat more timid three, the Carolina wren, the wren I know best because of its voluble ubiquity, rarely chooses to pack up and go. (Louisiana figures in its scientific name because that state provided the specimen from which the first formal description was made.) The same bird—not just the same species but the very same bird—may be found in the same home territory in every season. Once settled in, it may venture at most around the corner or across the street or, prodded by some yen for adventure, may even relocate to a brushpile, a hedgerow, or a shed as much as half a mile away. The bird is not much given to experiment except, on occasion, in its choice of nesting sites: a flower pot, a mailbox, one of the tattered old sneakers the Chief left on the deck, the bottom of a bathing suit hung out on the clothesline.

No matter the season, wherever a Carolina wren may establish its full-breasted self, it sings and sings. From dawn to dusk, first light to last faint glimmering, right lustily it sings and keeps on singing. And the ringing triplets, the resounding doublets issue from its throat as readily in frigid winter as they do in balmy spring or summer's heat. Nor is the bird bashful, but puts on its plumply clamorous display from myrtle twig or porch railing or the hood of the Chief's car. Two syllables or three, trilled, yodeled, embellished with intricately melismatic passages, the song is always melodious— and always loud. And it is a most perplexing mystery, how a bird the size of a penny whistle can sing a song large enough to fill a concert hall.

Sometimes, however, the Chief and I would like to do away with Carolina wrens, banish them all from the face of this earth, or perhaps send them back to Louisiana. Not gunshot nor thunderclap nor the shout of a Valkyrie is more galvanic than a wren making sudden utterance from the sill of an open window two feet about our sleeping heads. And, crash, there go the night's last and sweetest dreams, shattered beyond all possible repair by—mind you—a bird, a damnable bird with all stops pulled out and voice at full throttle.

The instrument on which the Carolina wren plays all its tunes is the syrinx. And every other songbird is similarly equipped. An organ unique to birds, it is the equivalent of the human larynx with its vocal cords. (Birds also possess a larynx, but one that lacks the sound-producing cords.) Though a few families, such as that of the whippoorwills and their kin, are fitted out with two syringes, most songsters have but one. That single syrinx is quite enough, depending on the species, to make sounds ranging from the bizarre to the sublime, from the rusty, tuneless creaks of the common grackle and the faint, breathless whistles of a cedar waxwing to a mockingbird's elaborate mimicry and the echoing, heart-haunting triplets of a wood thrush. In most birds, the syrinx is located like a slightly bulbous, upside-down Y-connector at the point that the trachea meets the two bronchial tubes. Pairs of muscles are attached to the outside of the syrinx; inside, it contains elastic membranes. Air forced from the lungs upward through the bronchi makes the membranes vibrate, creating sound. Pitch, tone, volume, rhythm—all may be altered by variations in air pressure and in the workings of the paired muscles. Nor does the bird need to open its bill for song to pour forth; unlike human sounds, syrinx music does not need to find resonance in oral cavities. And, *mirabile dictu,* because each side of the syrinx is independent of the other and under the separate control of one of the brain's two hemispheres, a single bird may set up harmonic vibrations or even sing two different songs at once. Not all syringes are alike, however. They come in several designs, from economy models with only a few attached muscles to a top-of-the-line version with eight or nine muscle pairs (the number depends, I'm told, on which expert in avian anatomy is doing the counting). Some birds, such as vultures, have no syrinx at all. Every songbird, however, has been granted the most intricate design, the one supplied with the maximum number of muscle pairs. Yet, though these birds are blessed with equal equipment, the uses to which it's put vary widely. Some birds present magnificent serenades, and others manage just a coo, a fretful buzzing, or a grating squawk.

But these facts are merely the scientific frosting on a story that has a mythic dimension. It might be said that deity is responsible for giving Carolina wrens and all other songbirds, sweet-singing or not, the instrument on which they play their tunes. And not just any old deity, but one much given to leering, butt-pinching, making lewd comments, and otherwise harassing nubile nymphs. The story is told by the Latin poet Ovid.

Once in the long-ago days of the gods, when everything was sacred and anything was possible, there lived a wood nymph named Syrinx. A devotee of Artemis, she emulated the goddess in chastity and dedication to the hunt. And anyone who saw her clad in hunting dress, bearing a quiver of arrows and a great bow made of horn, might reasonably think that he'd been granted a glimpse of the goddess herself. One day, as Syrinx returned from pursuing a stag, the god Pan, goat-footed and shaggy, accosted her and tried to cozy up with heavy-handed compliments: My dear, you look just like a goddess! Knowing full well what he was up to, and wanting none of him, Syrinx fled. Pan gave chase and caught up with her as she arrived at the reed-guarded bank of a marshy river. She cried to her sisters the river nymphs for help, and when Pan seized her, he found that he grasped nothing more than an armful of reeds. Nor was there any way to tell which single reed had once been Syrinx. Bleating in frustration, Pan tore at the reeds and broke off a bundle. And as his rough breath passed through their hollow stems, it was channeled into a sweet and melancholy plaint. Though he'd forever lost the object of his lust, he had found some consolation in music—and the wind instrument on which it might be played. In grudging admiration for the prey that had eluded him, Pan named his discovery the syrinx. But today the nymph is forgotten, and her name, which originally referred to a reed or a reedlike tube, is ignored by all but the ornithologists (and the doctors, who use it in the form *syringe*). People do, however, still acknowledge the capering goat-god. They call his primitive instrument the panpipe and eagerly (alas, how the mighty have fallen) buy tapes and CDs that feature the panpipe's only current virtuoso, Zamfir, playing romantic kitsch.

With a syrinx, with the voice of a divine nymph—that's *how* the wren sings. But there's nothing kitschy about its arias, and nothing remotely mythic either, especially not that high C hurled at dawn to pierce our innocent dreams. What, though, does the wren say when it sings? Or, as the field guides might put it, when its cheery teakettle wheedles and wheedles?

At one time, not many years ago, I was ambushed by the notion that each Carolina wren had a signature song. Members of the species might look alike, at least to my indiscriminating eyes, and to my unperceptive ears it seemed that, though their songs all employed the same characteristic syllabic patterns, no two wrens pronounced the syllables in precisely the same way. Thus, the wren that sang *peashooter* was not the wren that shouted *trickier* nor the wren that insisted on *me-too,* and if only I could attach its particular phrasing to each bird, then I'd be able to tell one wren from another. Not so. Once again, I'd succumbed to the human propensity to interpret all phenomena in terms intelligible to my own species. But this delusion fell away when, one September afternoon, wren song bubbled from a hedgerow. Couched deep in shadow, the bird was whisper-singing, and softly, blissfully it sang every last phrasing in the repertoire and then some. Since then, I've been aware that wrens may sometimes behave like dueling banjos, flinging the same music back and forth, as if to say, "I can sing *teakettle* better than you can."

I've come to respect *teakettle, cheery,* and the like as truly useful approximations of Carolina wren song. These words convey its character by imitating the number of notes to be repeated and also by suggesting its upbeat brightness, its very real cheer. Such verbal renditions are easier for most of us to understand than the pictures of sound, the oscillograms, that appear in some field guides and look (at least, to me) like hasty, up-and-down shadings made with a number-two pencil. It's our ears, after all, that apprehend music, not our eyes. Recordings of bird song thus provide much better tutelage than silent pages possibly can. But even recordings fall short of the real thing. As with any concert, the most intense, most informative pleasure comes from being on the spot to hear the song while beholding the singer.

In thicket and hedgerow, brushpile and border, from windowsill or shed roof, the Carolina wren makes lively, if exasperating, music. And every wren, Diver and Leaper alike, energetically gives voice. And every song contains some meaning—a claim to territory, a call to courtship, perhaps even a little bit of bragging. I'll never be able, however, to tell one kind of utterance from another, not any more than I can recognize a single wren amid the myriad. But every song sung by a wren, indeed every sound that it makes, contains one basic element that I understand absolutely, and I understand it because my own noises make the identical statement.

It should go without saying, then, that what the wren really says is simply, *I am.*

A Small
and Most Particular King

Two woodpeckers are at play, swooping, soaring at high speed through aerial games in the upper reaches of the longleaf pines. Or they seem to play, though they may more truly be engaged in the serious business of seeking food. But sport is suggested by the easy and companionable vigor of their movements. Follow the leader, tag, and chase, round and about—it certainly looks as if these two little black and white birds are having a great deal of fun up there amid the grey-brown branches and the green needles that are a full foot in length. Nor does the fact that there are watchers on the ground below give them the slightest pause. They appear unaware of our presence, our wide-eyed, scarcely breathing human presence.

It's the end of April, shirtsleeve weather, and honeysuckle has begun to sweeten the air. On this last Saturday of the month, at least a dozen people gathered to spend the morning listening to and participating in dicussions on environmental topics that ranged from water quality to wetlands. Then, after we'd gorged ourselves on seafood chowder, clam fritters, and fried fish, after we'd leaned against the well-shaded picnic tables for a calm half hour while a storyteller spun yarns about maritime life on this Carolina coast, the calls to action sounded: Birds! Canoes! Wildflowers! One and all, rousing ourselves from the ate-too-much impulse to cap off listening to stories with a good long nap, we joined the afternoon field-trip groups for which we'd signed up earlier. I'd chosen birds, of course. And off I went with seven others for an expedition into the Croatan National Forest.

Two o'clock in the afternoon is not usually an ideal time of day to look for birds. From late morning till about four in the afternoon, in any season, they're given to taking siestas. But on this Saturday, despite the time of day, the time of year is in our favor: The birds are courting, staking out nesting territories, and doing so at the top of their lungs. And the leaders of our trip, an attorney with the Southern Environmental Law Center and a consultant in botany and ornithology to the state's Natural Heritage Program, are both topnotch birders. Both, however, have cautioned us not to expect a glimpse of what we'd all most dearly like to see—the red-cockaded woodpecker. We may hope, yes, but we'd better not expect.

The shining blue afternoon and the Croatan are lavish with birds—two species of tyrant flycatchers and two of vireos, a redheaded woodpecker, a pair of red-shouldered hawks, and seven species of warblers, from bold parulas to a reclusive Swainson's. Treetops to understory, the action is plentiful, swift, continuous, and loud with overspilling song. With such abundance, it's impossible not to feel well-rewarded. Then rarity presents itself not in a single species but in two.

Just after 5:00 P.M., we head down Caleb Branch Road to Forest Service Road 199 and an extensive area of longleaf pine–wire grass savannah, the one and only kind of habitat in which the red-cockadeds nest. The social organization of these woodpeckers is like that of an extended family, and all join in—siblings and cousins, aunts and uncles—to excavate the nesting cavity that will be used by the colony's breeding pair. The work of excavation demands much time and energy, for the birds drill the nest not in easily yielding deadwood but in the living wood of a select few species of southern pines, including the longleaf. Not only must the chosen tree have reached full maturity, but its heartwood must be infected with a fungus disease, known as red heart, which makes the tree's hard core more amenable to drilling. Nevertheless, one such job may occupy a colony for several years. Almost as soon as work begins, the site of any excavation is announced by the pine sap that oozes from the hole in a sluggish but thick stream and dries frosty-white on the tree's trunk. To support itself, an active colony needs an area of open pine-wire grass savannah about a mile and a half in diameter.

A mile and a half! That translates to more than a thousand acres for under a dozen small birds. Nor are the red-cockaded woodpeckers like fish crows, Carolina wrens, or even their large cousins the pileated woodpeckers, all of which are birds on the increase, most likely because they're able to adapt to change. When one sort of habitat fails, they move with great success into another and often push the customary boundaries of their ranges into brand-new territories. But the red-cockadeds are specialists and birds of narrow, unbreakable habit. Their choice is, live in the pine savannah or die. But the open stands of mature pines in the Southeast have dwindled because of the trees' great commercial value as providers of naval stores—turpentine, rosin, and the like—and as a source of strong wood for construction. As the old pines in the Southeast disappear, so do the little woodpeckers. And, with insufficient habitat, their breeding pattern also works against them. Unlike most other species, not all adult red-cockadeds make the effort to reproduce each year; like maiden aunts and bachelor uncles, they share the life of the colony by serving the mated pair. It may be that these birds now endangered are wholly doomed.

Two lifelines, however, may exist—if it's not already too late to throw them out. One, in conjunction with preservation of existing stands, is the intentional planting of pines that would be allowed to mature. Nor would trees infected with red-heart fungus be felled in the name of preventing disease. The other tactic for rescue, more immediate but also more speculative, would be to speed up the nest-excavating process and, concomitantly, the arrival of new generations. The technique was born of 1989's Hurricane Hugo, which flattened thousands on thousands of acres of South Carolina's woodpecker pines, and with them, more active nests than anyone wanted to lose. In this case, it was not necessity but despair that mothered invention, and people concerned about the homeless little birds decided to make a desperate experiment: They drilled nestlike holes in living trees. And—miracle!—those red-cockaded woodpeckers moved right in.

Amid woodpecker pines that touch the sky like soft green brushes on the ends of long, grey handles, we linger in the Croatan as Saturday afternoon winds toward evening. The trees in active or former use are easy to identify. Not only do the bird-drilled entrance holes weep slow but copious quantities of sap, but the guardians of the Croatan, the rangers of the U.S. Forest Service, have ringed the trunks of these pines with wide bands of light blue paint. Five trees in the stand at which we gaze intently wear the significant color.

"Tree farthest back—head in the hole!" The low, urgent voice is that of one of the field trippers, a novice like me.

"Southern flying squirrel," says our attorney-guide without lifting his binoculars. Our consultant-guide, a man much given to taxonomic formality, says, "When a cavity's not in use, often *Glaucomys volans* moves in."

I can see without binoculars that the creature's posture in the entrance hole is not that of a bird. It looks more like a curious person leaning on the sill of an upper-story window to see what's going on out there in the neighborhood. And some law of natural economy is working here: Nothing goes to waste. The home vacated by birds for better or worse has found a new tenant. We look at the little rodent for a few more minutes, then move on.

And in another stand of mature longleaf pines, just across a ditch filled with pitcher plants in lush dark-red bloom, we hear bird song. With loud-ringing sweetness, the singer trills from the upper branches of a pine, and trills, and trills again.

"*Aimophila aestivalis,*" says our consultant-guide. His voice holds a note of surprised pleasure. Translating, our attorney-guide says, "Bachman's sparrow, come-and-go species. You don't always find them here. In fact, they're becoming rather scarce."

I spot it as it moves from branch to branch—warm brown with a rusty cap, long tail, no wing bars. The bird's not exciting to look at, but oh, his song is glorious. And this is spring, the song a part of reproductive ritual. I hope another sparrow is listening—not only listening but responding.

"Look, look, look! Two of 'em, yonder."

My eyes follow the pointing finger, but I don't see "them." No need, though, to ask what "they" are.

"One just went over the road. Oops, there goes the other."

Suddenly, I do see them. The pines on the road's other side are more widely spaced. Up there, near the treetops, they put on a fine aerial display. Land and take off, dive and soar, whatever they do, these small, quick, black and white birds move, so it seems, with an utterly blithe assurance. And the black and white barred wings and backs, the white, white cheeks, almost reverse the black-cheek, white-back color pattern of their close kin the downy and hairy woodpeckers. Perhaps it's the lateness of the day, the near-dusk hour, that intensifies the whiteness of those cheeks and makes them gleam. None of us can see if either bird wears the cockade for which the species is named. It's the tiny red stripe that the male wears at the top of his white cheek—so tiny that even at close range it would be almost as hard to spot as the minuscule red patch on an eastern kingbird's crown. The gender of these birds is concealed from us, and there's more that we cannot know. Are they old or young? Part of a colony or simply a lone and maybe lonesome pair? The warm light of the westering sun gives a shine to the dark green needles of the longleaf pines. All that we do know for certain is that two small woodpeckers—two representatives of an endangered species—are here and alive at this place in the Croatan Forest and so, most thankfully, are we.

Later, of course, I look for more information.

"Red-cockaded woodpecker—every forester's nightmare," says a young man entering his senior year in forestry at North Carolina

State. How so? I ask, and he explains. "You got a choice—manage for timber, manage for birds. Birds are okay for government agencies that don't get their money by cutting trees. But when the government says you can't cut trees, the individual who has to make a living off them suffers." Longleaf pines reach a size for harvesting before they attain the age that makes them attractive to the little birds. And he shows me a longleaf seedling in what's called its grass stage, a bushy spray of needles, green and pliable as grass, that surrounds a fat white bud the size of a bantam's egg. It's clear that he loves that nascent tree. His hand gently gathers and strokes the soft needles.

The red-cockaded woodpecker is, in his view, the Southeast's equivalent of the Northwest's northern spotted owl that now keeps loggers out of many old-growth forests. In the Southeast, almost no acreage suitable for this woodpecker now remains in private hands— the trees have long ago been harvested. But the South's publicly protected woodlands, such as the Croatan and the Apalachicola National Forest in Florida, are theaters, courtrooms, battlefields for another enactment of the old conflict—the economic interests of the human community versus the presence of another form of life that has as full a right as we do to exist—if, that is, a right may spring from the simple fact that we *are* here on this earth. And all of us, of whatever species, are here, but—and this is the important part—not of our own volition or doing.

But what if a species now living becomes extinct? I ask the young man what he thinks might happen if the "forester's nightmare" were to disappear.

He doesn't reply right away. Then he shakes his head and says quietly, "I don't know. Something."

That question—*what happens?*—makes me uncomfortable too. Thinking about the proposition is like looking into the bottomless well of space. Talking about it can be like attacking deeply held belief: birds or trees, which better serve humankind? And just about everybody knows the answer to that one: It doesn't count unless you can take it to the bank.

I put the question to the Croatan's wildlife biologist: "What happens if the red-cockadeds vanish? What consequences would we face?" He has just told me the happy news that one of the birds was spotted earlier this year in a section of the forest that's only fourteen miles from Great Neck Point. The part of the Croatan in which I'd seen the birds lies fifty long miles away. This close-to-home section turns out to be located in the immediate vicinity of the open longleaf woodlands in which I spent a grey and frigid New Year's morning with Betty, my deer-hunting friend.

"What happens? On a day-to-day basis, we're not affected," he says. "It takes a lifetime, several lifetimes, for the costs to show."

The red-cockaded woodpeckers, as he explains, are only one part, a small but much publicized part, of the pine-wire grass ecosystem on which many species are utterly dependent. The singer of heart-breaking sweetness, Bachman's sparrow, is among the more obvious, and it is joined by a host of cryptic others, flowers, insects, the red-heart fungus. The Croatan is now being managed to perserve existing stands of mature pines and to restore the system to some of its former domain. The expensive, perhaps impossible, struggle has been mounted not merely to save an endangered woodpecker but to reverse the downslide of an entire system. If one part is lost, the system itself may fail. The biologist speaks then of the web, the interconnectedness, of life, but says it's a whole lot stickier than anything a spider spins. And he says, "Whatever you do now gets paid back sooner or later. Mother Nature keeps track."

Again and again, mind's eye observes two little black and white woodpeckers playing at high games in the April sunlight and the glistening green shadows of tall old pines.

High games, high stakes: What will become of *Picoides borealis,* the bird that resembles Picus, the bird of the north? The red-cockaded woodpecker does not appear on eighteenth-century lists of American birds, and its actual Southeastern range was misidentified as boreal by the ornithologist Vieillot, who named the species and published its first description in 1807. The bird's history, however, is truly, regally ancient, dating back to a mythic time. The name of its genus acknowledges its direct descent from the aboriginal wood-pecker, Picus the king, who reigned in Italy before there was a Rome. He forfeited his human shape, became a bird with feathers of royal red and gold and a sturdy hammer bill, because he'd rejected the love of Circe, the same vengeful enchantress who'd turned

Odysseus's men to swine. From this one ancestor, all the world's more than two hundred species of woodpeckers have evolved. An extensive tribe, they share a noble pedigree and a royal past. Most of them also share sanguine prospects for the future. The one king is dead, long live the many. And most of them still reign in their hereditary kingdoms. But the red-cockaded has come perilously close to losing the country it was born to, and there's nowhere else to go. What will become of this small and most particular king?

What, for that matter, will become of us?

The Musical Shuttle

No trespassing! A mockingbird dives straight at Sally Doberman's rump but pulls out and up a split second before making
contact. Though Sal pays the bird no mind as she trots down the
lane, the strafing maneuver has succeeded splendidly from the bird's
point of view: An invader of its territory has been repelled.

Northern mockingbirds—what feisty, show-off, me-first creatures! And they're as close to fearless as any wild bird can be. They
choose exposed, eye-level perches in shrubs and on electric wires or   65

clothesline poles. Strutting with cocked tails on open lawns (where anything might pounce), they perform insouciant courtship and territory-claiming displays; with an almost mechanical precision, the tails fan out to show white edges, the pearl-grey wings lift and fold, revealing, hiding, revealing a dazzle of white flash patches. Year-round, mockers are passionately territorial, nor does it matter what species, avian or otherwise, may have got there first. All mockers are fierce to defend whatever they claim. Sometimes, it's sufficient room to breed; sometimes, assuring and guarding a food supply. And beware the adults from late spring through summer, for it is then that they zero in most aggressively on any possible threat. The objective, of course, is protection of the young birds that huddle in the nest or, fully fledged but still dependent, hide in the shrubbery and hiss with insistently begging *seep-seep-seep* calls for parental attention. I also suspect that mockers grab space just for the hell of it, for the sheer, flapdoodling fun of chasing away all that dare cross the invisible boundary that separates the bird's kingdom from everything else. Mockers rush at errant intruders and drive them away from feeders, from favorite perches, from the black gum tree when it's laden with enough berries to sate every fruit-eating bird at Great Neck Point. Mockers dive with regularity on innocent canine rumps. They even run along porch railings to peck at the outstretched tail of a snoozing cat. Then, as if this kind of pushiness were not enough, the bird cusses—*tschak!* Loud, harsh, rude, the note sounds like a snort of disgust combined with a hawking of phlegm. In the mockers' favor, it must be said that the objects of their fury are never hurt. Aggression seems an end in itself, an exercise meant to discharge pent-up energy before it bursts of its own overheated accord. Full of chutzpah and prima-donna arrogance, the bird is a snob, a bully, a tyrant conducting a reign of terror over more timorous species. One neighbor, who has made her yard a paradise of feeders, is so outraged that mockers drive away "her" chickadees, sparrows, and finches that she intentionally flouts the laws protecting songbirds and wages a summer-long search-and-destroy campaign on mocker nests. Her efforts, themselves outrageous, are luckily like those of King Canute, who attempted to stay the incoming tide by royal command. It's equally impossible for mere humanity to stem the reproductive urge. The adult birds simply find a new nest-construction site and raise another generation to strut, cuss, and chase off intruders—and give endless concerts.

Oh listen! A mockingbird sings, and the song is not equalled for beauty by any other bird on earth, not wren nor thrush nor legendary nightingale. And those who listen have long been moved to put their wonder into words. The English naturalist John Lawson, who issued his list of Carolina avifauna in 1709, calls mockingbirds "the choristers of America" and says that though they may be bred in captivity and caged as songsters, he prefers to listen to them singing in his fruit trees, in which they yearly build their nests. Another Englishman, Mark Catesby, who published a lavishly illustrated *Natural History of Carolina, Florida, and the Bahama Islands* in several volumes between 1731 and 1743, says this of the mocker:

From March till August it sings incessantly night and day with the greatest variety of notes; and, to complete his compositions, borrows from the whole choir, and repeats to them their very own tunes with such artful melody, that it is equally pleasing and surprising. They may be said not only to sing but dance, by gradually raising themselves from the place where they stand, with their wings extended, and falling with their head down to the same place; then turning around, with their wings continuing to spread, have many pretty antic gesticulations with their melody.

Fifty years later, in 1791, William Bartram, an American botanist and close observer of all wild things, provides a reason for the dance and its "antic gesticulations": The bird "bounds aloft with the celerity of an arrow, as it were to recover or recall his very soul, expired in the last elevated strain" of song.

But it is a poet, not a naturalist, who seems to have listened best of all—Walt Whitman, who gathered images and poured them forth in poems the way a mocker gathers sounds and spills them out in cascades of song: "Out of the cradle endlessly rocking, Out of the mockingbird's throat, the musical shuttle. . . ." And from the shuttle, threads of melody and harmony ply swift between the great, multifarious, infinitely protean warp provided by the mocker's world.

Mockingbirds belong to the Mimidae, the mimic thrushes, a family found only in the Americas. Two other far more modest and retiring members of the family haunt the woods and hedgerows of the Point—grey catbird and brown thrasher. The catbird's binomial speaks of its favored habitat: *Dumetella carolinensis,* Carolina bird of the little bramble thickets. The thrasher's binomial makes note of its appearance: *Toxostoma rufum,* reddish-brown bird with bill that curves like an archer's bow. As for the mocker, attention focuses— where else?—on the voice: *Mimus polyglottos,* mimic speaking many tongues. Though the polyglot mimic is the only one that flaunts itself in public places, all are equally able to spin out glorious tunes. A catbird hidden in the dimness of a brushy tangle sings sotto voce, the notes bubbling forth without repetition. Catbirds' songs seem mostly of their own devising, with only the merest, occasional hint of wren or pine warbler coming through. Thrashers' compositions are also original, little or no imitation here, and the often doubled phrases of their singing are never shouted out in mocker style but delivered in clear, sweet melodic lines that shine like silver wire. Though field guides have it that the thrasher sings from a high, exposed perch, the Point's birds usually make chamber music in the shady recesses of a hedgerow and give concerts from center stage at only one time of year, the brief early-summer interval between the fledging of the first brood and the starting of the next. It is as if this singing from an open perch celebrates success and asks that it recur. Mockers, of course, are onstage and up front all the time, both day and night, from one spring nonstop right into the next. Mockers invent, copycat, and plagiarize. They manage to acknowledge every sound they hear, and the acknowledgment is like that of classical Roman practice, in which a poet would pay homage to admired colleagues or predecessors by tucking some of their best-crafted lines into his own poems. And in the choices—what to mimic, what to parody, what to produce with grand bel canto agility from the loftiest realms of avian inspiration—and also in the arrangements of these elements, the mocker's music is no less original than, say, a symphony that incorporates a medley of folk songs.

Listen to the mockingbird! If there were contests at Great Neck Point to determine which species produces the greatest quantity of song—not simply sound but song—mocker would surely vie with

Carolina wren. All songbirds are capable of uttering sounds—chips, calls, scolds—at any time of year. For most of them, however, song peals forth only when daylight begins to lengthen and avian gonads swell, making it urgent that territories be claimed for purposes of reproduction. Almost always, it's the male bird that sings a musical fence around the chosen ground. But after nesting is under way, such loud advertisement of territorial bounds often comes to a halt, and a protective silence sets in. But not with the mockers, not with the wrens. Year-round, month in and month out, they sing. And in the imagined contest, I think that mockers would easily win. Wrens sing from daybreak to dusk, but mockers make themselves heard not only during daylit hours but in the black-silk hours of the night. The male mocker does the musical honors in the nesting season, which usually includes two broods. Then, when the young are fully fledged and on their own, the female also lifts her tuneful voice. (I'm tempted to let the anthropomorphic view sneak in and say that she's deservedly whooping it up now that the kids have left home.) In quantity of song—in its surges and cascades and torrents—no bird can outdo the mocker.

Quality is something else. The medley offered by any one bird seems to depend on the bums and aristocrats with which it's been associating. Listen to the mockingbird and know, as well, whether it's taken up territory near the riverfront or claimed a homestead close to the woods. If the bird squeals gull talk or gargles like a boat-tailed grackle, it's been hanging out down at the shore. The bird that's settled itself farther inland knows how to speak titmouse and cardinal and jay. It may carol like a wren or bark like a squirrel or—I heard it once—imitate a chain saw.

Mocker song pours loudest and most insistent, of course, during the weeks of assuring a nesting territory. From late spring well into August's dog days, there's always a mocker or three posting melodies to warn off trespassers. And cautionary song is backed up with the aggressive tactics of flap, lunge, and strafe. But near the autumnal equinox, when most pairs have completed the haggard work of rearing not just one brood but two, there seems to be a temporary halt in the vocal acrobatics. Come fall, however, come the first cool night that's followed by a clear blue day, the singing starts again.

Both males and females perform right merrily, though the music is sometimes tentative, as if the singer were either an amateur or so badly out of practice that all it can do is sound some ragged, off-key scales. And sometimes the song sounds hoarse, as if the bird has not quite recovered from a summer's worth of operatic shouting. And still another style of mocker music flows with such sublimity that celestial choirs might well take lessons. I've heard it in every season, but it seems to find voice most often when the leaves of the Virginia creeper turn red in mid-October. Nor is it an anthem, a hosanna rendered forte. No, it's whisper-song. Every imitation and every invention in the repertoire is there but sung pianissimo and sung with such delicate joy that it's quite clear the bird is singing to and for itself.

Oh, listen! And many people can. Though song and story associate the bird with Southern belles and Southern heat, with sweet Hallie sleeping in her grave where the weeping willows wave, and with the death of innocence in Harper Lee's undying tale *To Kill a Mockingbird*, the mocker has never been a bird of strictly Confederate habitat but is widespread and common through most of the United States. In recent years, its range has expanded north across the border into Canada.

Yet it's rumored that the mocker is in trouble, and not just the parochial trouble created by Great Neck Point's own Queen Canute, who'd halt the local tides of reproduction. Though mockingbirds may have increased their numbers elsewhere, North Carolina's population is reported to have decreased by an alarming forty-five percent.

Reasons for the rise and fall of bird populations can often be pinpointed. Some of the trends in North Carolina head happily upward—those for the purple martin, the pileated woodpecker, and, perhaps most notably, the eastern bluebird, up an astounding 369 percent in the last twenty years. Such a beneficent explosion was triggered by widespread provision of man-made housing—bluebird boxes by the tens of thousands—which has more than offset a scarcity of natural nesting holes. On the downside, one classic reason for swift decreases in population can be found in the use of DDT-type pesticides, which nearly extirpated eagles, osprey, pelicans, and others; though some chemically diminished species are still a long way from recovery, the banning of such pesticides in North America has led to an almost miraculous recovery for many of our affected birds. The same, alas, cannot be said of many countries elsewhere, which continue to use materials toxic to birds as well as bugs. And, though North American birds are no longer threatened by chlorinated hydrocarbons, it's possible that other sorts of chemicals are working mischief here. Then, the downward trends in the numbers of some neotropical species, such as eastern kingbirds and some of the wood warblers that breed in North Carolina but winter in Central and South America, have been legitimately ascribed to loss of their hibernal rain-forest habitat. And loss of summer habitat right here at home—the felling of the woods in which they breed—may be a greater, more insidious cause of their decline. More insidious because it's easier and more convenient to point a finger at the distant tropics than blame ourselves, but, according to a hot new study made by a researcher at Dartmouth College, we are the major culprits. It's Pogo Possum all over again: "We have seen the enemy, and he is us." (Now all we need do is recognize the villain in the mirror.) What happens is that land development can chop forests into tracts too small to support a breeding pair and shrink cover to such an extent that birds that otherwise might have reared more of their kind are made easy prey for foxes, hawks, and cats. Nonmigratory birds, such as the bobwhite and the rufous-sided towhee, also face shortages of living space because of development or changed agricultural practices.

But the mocker—the quintessential yard bird if ever there was one—should profit from development, which after all creates even more yards in which the bird can strut and sing. Why then would an increase in yards see a decrease in a species fond of suburban amenities? Yards offer shrubs in which to nest, along with porch railings and TV antennas from which to holler and yodel and carol polyglot song. Yards provide an abundance of strolling dogs and sleeping cats to pester and legions of other birds to terrorize. What more could a mocker ask? Of course, I inquire how it can be that the Tarheel State seems to be suffering a grievous and most peculiar attrition in its mockingbird population. It turns out that no one has definitive answers, but I'm offered an assorted batch of speculations.

Before these speculations are handed on, it may be well to take a brief look at the method used in this case to determine avian populations. The North American Breeding Bird Survey, sponsored cooperatively by the U.S. Fish and Wildlife Service and the Canadian Wildlife Service, has been conducted across the continent every June since 1966. Each participant drives a predetermined twenty-five-mile route and pauses for three minutes every half mile to look, listen, and jot the names of every species seen or heard. Because birds reveal their presence more often to the ear than to the eye, the task demands not only keen hearing but an encyclopedic knowledge of songs and calls.

And the first speculation comes from the man who coordinates North Carolina's Breeding Bird Survey and also serves as a zoologist for the state's Natural Heritage Program, which catalogues flora and fauna and assesses their scarcity or abundance. He says, "When you clear a forest and put in houses and yards, you should have more mockingbirds as well as robins. I don't know what's going on with these birds." He does, however, put forth a guess—air pollution and poisoning by fertilizers. But the puzzle remains: Why should North Carolina's robins flourish where its mockers fail?

Two friends arrive independently at another, most villainous reason for the mocker's decline. As one of them puts it: "Cats. Development equals people equals pets equals cats. And cats kill birds."

Attrition is not, hallelujah, evident at the Point. I hope that it never will be. But the voice of Walt Whitman rises. Singing his own patchwork song, plying his boisterous, onrolling dactyls to weave into a single fabric hundreds on hundreds of disparate images, he offers an unwitting caution at the end of a great poem's first stanza:

> Out of the cradle endlessly rocking,
> Out of the mockingbird's throat, the musical shuttle,
> Out of the Ninth-month midnight, . . .
> I, chanter of pains and joys, uniter of here and hereafter, . . .
> A reminiscence sing.

To my ear, the significant, scary word is *reminiscence.* In the poem's next stanza, he tells in pictures that are both audible and fragrant what it is that he remembers from one long-gone May on his native Long Island, which he calls Paumanok:

Once Paumanok,
When the lilac-scent was in the air and Fifth-month grass was
    growing,
Up this seashore in some briers,
Two feather'd guests from Alabama, two together,
And their nest, and four light-green eggs spotted with brown,
And every day the he-bird to and fo near at hand,
And every day the she-bird crouch'd on her nest, silent, with
    bright eyes,
And every day I, a curious boy, never too close, never disturbing
    them,
Cautiously peering, absorbing, translating.

But one day, suddenly, the she-bird is gone. Her mate makes lament. And, looking back, the grown man understands that as "a curious boy," he was first challenged by the need to come to terms with death.

Reminiscence—a melancholy word. It evokes thoughts of fragility and evanescence. It suggests loss and makes ongoing attempts to save all that's gone glimmering by keeping it bright in memory—so long, that is, as memory itself is able to endure. The word bids me try to be careful lest my actions lead to loss and then to recollections of a reality that no longer exists. The mocker deserves far better than becoming a subject for such despairing reminiscence.

And then, oh then, another speculation: "I think the forty-five percent is wrong. We're probably looking at little or no decline." Breaking through the gloom like a mocker's full-throated song in the dark of night, this opinion comes from a professional bird-watcher, an ornithologist who has made the definitive study of his country's birds and who makes his living as a consultant to public agencies and private organizations that focus on wildlife. His current project is to survey certain rare or endangered species—Bachman's sparrow, the red-cockaded woodpecker—for the Natural Heritage Program. When such a respectable authority as he believes that we've lost few mockingbirds, or none at all, I listen attentively and ask for his reasons. He answers with one word: development.

But when he elaborates, his equation does not end with cats. It goes this way: Development equals cleared land equals routes with fewer birds of real interest to the skilled observer-listeners who make the official Breeding Bird Surveys. These people, he thinks, have abandoned the now-tame routes where mockers may be tallied and have moved on to wilder stretches of road where more elusive species may skulk but never a polyglot mimic is heard or seen. And he adds that the possibility of error in the North Carolina surveys is compounded by a paucity of survey routes and teams to cover them; the samplings are so random, slim, and nonrepresentative that any statistics using such data are sadly, inevitably skewed.

I hope he's right. If he is, it would seem that the diminishment of the mockingbird population is a phenomenon of appearances, not substance, and that it has two causes. One is the stubborn human preference for the exotic over the mundane. The other is a far from uncommon accident of impercipience, which might generally be called the falling-tree problem: When a tree falls to earth, does the impact create any sound at all if nobody's there to hear it? Restated in mockingbird terms, does the bird exist if *Homo sapiens* somehow fails to notice it? Of course it does.

There's good news, too, on the strictly local front: Queen Canute has had a change of heart. She still regards the mocker with implacable dislike, but she's forsworn the destruction of any more nests. The reason is that when she used a long-handled flounder gig to reach and dislodge a high nest, the eggs it contained broke when they hit the ground. And she found herself impaled on the sharp prongs of remorse.

May the mockingbird flourish. Next year, the year after, the decade and the century after that, may it prosecute all trespassers to the full extent of its self-confident fury. May it fly aloft with the speed of an arrow to recover the soul that it sent forth in song. And may the musical shuttle continue to weave the strands of its brazen, reverberant, most original mimicry through the world's green and wonderful warp.

The Flycatchers,
the Snake,
and the Biological Imperative

The rat snake is up a tree! It's a big 'un, probably the same specimen dressed in faintly pin-striped black that my husband the Chief and I have observed for the last two weeks as it lay at full six-foot stretch on the backyard grass beside the azaleas. Now, damned if it isn't fourteen feet up the loblolly pine that stands at the south end of the azalea patch. Strung out along a horizontal branch, the snake is eyeing the owl box tacked to the tree's trunk. The box is mere inches away from its stillness, its unblinking gaze.

Before the tale unfolds, it's worth taking a minute to look at that owl box—the scene of the action. A large box, about a foot high and constructed of cedar, its overt purpose is to furnish a pair of screech owls with a cozy nesting place. But the Chief and I know full well that it was made and presented to us with an ulterior motive. The young man who fashioned it was courting, trying to evoke my approbation by catering to my fancy for birds, and the reason for wanting to please me was that he hoped to marry my younger daughter. To this end, he also gave me a bluebird box, now set on a post in the backyard, and he sought the Chief's favor as well with many gifts: two pickup truckloads of manure—one of rabbit droppings, the other of horse apples—to enrich the soil of our vegetable garden; one truckload of polished but broken slabs of granite carefully selected from the scrap heap of a tombstone maker. The granite, mortared with cement mix and river sand, was used to build an outdoor fireplace—the only Roman ruin on North Carolina's wide and salty lower Neuse River. It takes much muscle to load granite and manure into a pickup, many hours to measure and build bird boxes. The gifts were thoughtful, generous, truly useful. The idea behind them, of course, was to stir the Chief and me to such a wild pitch of approval that we would support his matrimonial cause. That was four years ago. Today, the well-sweetened garden flourishes, the Roman ruin sends up fragrant smoke whenever the Chief makes offerings of mullet or pork chops to the flames, chickadees rear families in the bluebird house, and the young man has been happily married for the last three years, but not to my daughter. Owls, however, have never tenanted the box designed especially for them.

Instead, another species moved in. In late May the year before last, a pair of great crested flycatchers claimed it. We watched them from the yard or the kitchen window. It took them several weeks to furnish the place to their liking with crisp brown leaves, bits of dried grass, and a snakeskin, oh surely a snakeskin, though we never saw them carry one in. Throughout this stage of settling in, they held much conversation, calling to each other with a sound that seems to bear an enthusiastic urgency—*wheep! wheeeep!* After the nest was built, they went into seclusion for another few weeks. We saw them rarely as the eggs were laid and incubated. But when the eggs hatched and baby bills gaped wide with constant, imperious hunger, the parents made frequent flights to and fro, delivering food, going out to hunt for more. When the nestlings, three of them so far as I could count, fledged and left the box, we felt suddenly bereft—no backyard bustle for watching eyes, no cheerful calls for listening ears. The absence of flycatchers was almost palpable; we'd lost the pleasure of observation. Yet the emptiness of the yard was an emptiness that signified success: The pair had accomplished one of their lives' most basic tasks—the sending into the world of a new, strong generation. What better solace for our petty loss?

Year-round, various members of the family Tyrannidae, the tyrant flycatchers, ornament our rural enclave on the Neuse. Some breed here, some spend the winter, others merely pause for a day or three en route to somewhere else. The great cresteds are one of four different Tyrannidae that summer here to raise their young. There are also the elusive Acadian flycatchers, not much bigger than a chickadee, that I'm sometimes lucky enough to hear or see in densely tree-shadowed wetlands. Then the elegant, chittering eastern kingbirds build nests embellished with streamers of Spanish moss high in the loblollies close to the shore. Of all the family, they may be the most imperious, the most tyrannical; should an osprey enter the kingdom of a nesting pair, a tiny but furious ball of feathers will hurl itself into the air and deliver a nonstop string of regal invective as it chases the large intruder, sometimes riding on its back, for a distance as great as a quarter mile. Far more modest and retiring are the plaintively calling eastern wood peewees that construct nest cups on horizontal pine or hardwood branches and camouflage them so that they look not like a habitation but simply another clump of grey-green lichens. The only giveaway to the location of a peewee's nest is the bird's activity as it builds or as it feeds its young. In winter, all these species are supplanted by one, the eastern phoebe, which bobs its tail as it perches and frequently calls out, sometimes announcing its name quite precisely, but more often slurring the syllables into a briskly trilled *ph-BRRR*. As for the migrants that touch down only briefly—who knows what might appear? A few western kingbirds tend to show up during the last ten days of September, and once, just once, I saw a grey kingbird, common farther south, displaying itself on an electric wire.

Great crested flycatchers don't wear a crest like that of a cardinal or jay; instead, it looks as if the hand of creation had affectionately tousled their head feathers. But of all the Point's flycatchers, these crestless great cresteds are surely the jauntiest. The others, except for the western kingbird with a wash of yellow on its belly, are dressed in somber greys and blacks enlivened only by touches of white. Some, to be sure, wear a red spot atop their heads, but it's small and therefore rarely glimpsed. But great cresteds offer citrus and spice—tails the rust-red of cinnamon, bellies bright as sun-polished lemons. From earliest May well into September, these cheerful colors spring readily to the eye.

According to John James Audubon, the colors are the outer wrappings of an inbred and overweening ferocity. He comments thus on great-crested behavior: "Tyrannical perhaps in a degree surpassing the King Bird, it yet seldom chases the larger birds of prey, but, unlike the Bee Martin [another name for the kingbird], prefers attacking those smaller ones which inadvertently approach its nest or its station. Among themselves these birds have frequent encounters, on which occasions they shew an unrelenting fierceness almost amounting to barbarity. The *plucking* of a conquered rival is sometimes witnessed." And Audubon's portrait shows two males, the upper bird lording it over a vanquished rival with half of its tail feathers missing. The plucked feathers drift across the painting as if blown by a light breeze. Audubon seems to have portrayed the species and made his comments from direct observation, and though I've not yet been granted a look at these birds in a bellicose mood, the opportunity may come along.

For great crested flycatchers are far from reclusive. Like a good many other Tyrannidae, they flaunt their presence by perching in open places—electric wires, fences, clotheslines, the tips of leafless branches—from which they rise to snap up flying insects in their bills. Prey disposed of, they often settle back on the same perch or one nearby. But unlike some other flycatchers, great cresteds are almost as obvious in the sites they select for their nests. I've seen them rear young not only in our owl box but in a first-story, south-facing apartment in an otherwise unoccupied martin house and in a crevice at Mo's barn. The crevice, a handy happenstance, was formed by a flap of tarpaper peeling away from the barn's wood just under the peak of the roof. As a matter of course, great cresteds use a snakeskin as a nest's foundation, perhaps because its slight, scaly roughness gives purchase to the overlay of more delicate materials. (Some other species of some other families—titmice and blue grosbeaks among them—also show a preference for snakeskin foundations, though lately the grosbeaks have discovered a substitute in the form of discarded plastic, be it lunch bags or scraps of vinyl. But nests built on such new-fangled stuff have a tendency to slip their foundations in a strong wind; nest and nestlings land plop on the ground.) When it comes to choosing a snakeskin, it seems that not just any old castoff will do for a pair of great cresteds; one opaquely white skin peeked from the nest in the south-facing apartment while three more littered the grass below. Once they've discovered a suitable nesting site, great cresteds—the same pair? hard to tell—tend to use it the following year. The crevice at Mo's barn was given no second chance, for the tarpaper fell away, but the species had laid claim to the martin house, same apartment, the year before we found the rejected snakeskins on the ground.

Thus it was not unexpected that a pair of the birds would build a new nest in the owl box this year. But there was a surprise. Much activity around the box announced their interest. We thought at first that construction was under way. No. Deconstruction! Back and forth, those birds were entering the box with empty bills and emerging with straws or ragged leaves clamped in their mandibles. Not many species are such tidy housekeepers, sweeping out the old before the new is set in place. Some wrens are equally fastidious, but most other birds either build over last year's leavings or find a never-used location. Only after the flycatchers had thoroughly cleaned the box did they bring in fresh materials. And when the nest was completed, the eggs laid, the silence of brooding took over.

Until today. Just after the sun had crossed the meridian, the silence was broken. Nor was it a cheery *wheep!* that we heard but a concatenation of cries—rapid, chattering, almost hoarse. What on earth!

"I see it," the Chief says, looking out the kitchen window. "Snake by the box."

Out we run. On our arrival beneath the pine, the adult birds disappear. The big rat snake lies motionless.

"My *birds!*" I exclaim.

The Chief replies, "We might be able to get that snake. Birds or snake, what do you choose?"

A dilemma: My heart lies with the birds—they strike no dark chords in my appreciation of their kind—but my head understands that the snake is as innocent as they, for it has climbed the tree in guileless obedience to the mandate of its hunger. Birds and snake, all three are responding instinctively at this moment to the biological imperative, which is no more nor less than giving their individual genes a chance to survive, to be inherited. That the species also survives is merely the simple, unwitting, fortunate by-product of myriad separate efforts to win out over the competition. The imperative has two components, each of equal force: Eat to maintain life in a condition fit for breeding; breed so that the life of one's genes goes on. I think of a beam scale with a pan suspended at either end of a balanced rod. Because the weight of the imperative's twin components is identical, it's possible to imagine the pans in equilibrium. But imagination envisions an ideal impossible of attainment. Reality always and plainly tips the scales, and one component, doesn't matter which, is given added weight by circumstance or season. In this case, one pan contains the flycatchers' eggs, and the other holds the muscular hunger of the rat snake. Is it allowed to read cries of distress as calls for help?

Heart wins. "Birds."

But the snake, its instincts intent on dinner, is fourteen feet up that tree, and the shed yields no implement, not bush-axe nor rake, with a handle long enough to extend human reach to such a height. The Chief instructs me to fetch the new flounder gig that's leaning against the front deck, but even that long-handled instrument, meant to let us stand on the bulkhead and spear flounder as they lie on the riverbed seven feet below, cannot quite touch the snake's dark, slender body. Perhaps a hurled object will dislodge its ominous stillness. The sandy coast provides no rocks. So we gather pinecones and fallen sticks, throw them, and miss.

It's Saturday, a day of leisure. People start arriving in our backyard, adults, children, all alerted by the mysterious but normal osmotic process that lets the Point know almost instantly of any opportunity for diversion. Soon, grown-ups and kids are all pitching cones and sticks at the snake, which seems fastened to the branch by the strong glue of its hunger. Someone goes to the deserted lot next door, finds a piece of weathered brick, and sends it aloft. It hits! And elicits a lightning response. Instantly the snake ascends, climbing another twelve feet up the tree. It's farther from the nest but still within devouring range of those vulnerable eggs. What next?

"We need a gun," the Chief says. But he and I keep no such weapon on our premises.

I go inside to use the phone while the multitude in the yard stands vociferous snake-watch. The place to start looking for marksmanship is with our sharpshooting neighbor Lana, who just last month used her sixteen-gauge shotgun to blast away not only a snake but also her bluebird box. She's not at home. The second call succeeds: Our friend Cap'n Harry, a reserve deputy for the sheriff's office, will be right over with his .22. Voices from the yard let me know that the snake has slithered down to the branch beside the box. I rush outside. The snake is unperturbed; it seems sure of its meal. By the time Harry arrives, its head and six inches of its body are inside the box.

He fires. Nor does he miss. The rope of the snake's body lashes, its head withdraws from the box. He fires again. The reptile tumbles to the ground, and the tines of the new flounder gig are bloodied for the first time. The carcass is taken into the back field, where it will furnish food for other appetites—bacteria, ants, scavenging crows.

When the adult birds return to the box late in the afternoon and appear again on Sunday, and again the day after, I feel, despite a lingering unease, that our human interference has been justified.

But cries beseech us at noon on Tuesday. The scene is almost a rerun of the first. A second rat snake lies on the branch beside the box, not stretched out at full length like the first but wrapped in seemingly careless loops around the branch and around itself. It's a workday, so both Lana and Harry are beyond summoning, but we call the retired colonel of Marines who lives four doors downriver. He marches promptly to our yard, fires his rifle, and kills the snake, which turns out to be a relatively piddling four-footer.

This time the flycatchers do not return. Have they simply been frightened away? Or has this second visitant consumed their eggs, destroyed their young? At dusk four days later, we're given an answer. Yet a third rat snake has discovered the nest—not only dis-covered but entered it, most likely because it still contained something worth eating. All we can see is the snake's head and several inches of its body protruding from the box's entrance hole.

If I didn't know better, I'd swear that it's grinning.

Thirteen Ways
of Looking at a Grackle

The river is moving.
The blackbird must be flying.

WALLACE STEVENS,
Thirteen Ways of Looking at a Blackbird, XII

I

Among the four hilled rows newly planted with corn seed on
the north side of our garden, the only moving things are the blaze-
orange ribbons tied to wooden stakes and a small nylon wind sock
fashioned in the shape of a carp with red scales. Fish and ribbons
flutter in the lightest river breeze, and when the wind picks up force,
they answer with a rapid, rustling slap. Other gardens at the Point

are defended by pillowcase flags, streamers made of rags, or shiny aluminum pie pans strung on a line. We all hope, of course, that movement, noise, and sun-shot glitter will frighten the grackles away before they discover and seize the newly sprouted corn.

But how sharp, a grackle's eye! How swift and ruthless! Its pupil gleams darkly, a well without a bottom. Its yellow iris radiates the only light amid the blackness of the feathers. And in no more than a wink of time, the birds will learn that they've nothing to fear.

II

Quiscalus quiscula—what's in the common grackle's name? Most of the binomials applied to the birds are amenable to interpretation. They mean something, and they can easily be translated into English. But when it comes to the genus called *Quiscalus* and, more particularly, to the species denominated *quiscula*, the designers of formal bird names seem to have been engaged in an antic enterprise. And there is one taxonomist above all others, a certain Louis Jean Pierre Vieillot (1748–1831), to whom may be ascribed most of the credit—or blame—for these nonsensical *Q* words. What could have possessed Vieillot? A polysyllabic case of indecision? A let's-get-on-with-it haste? A sly wish to sow confusion? Or was he simply entertaining himself, taking a break from scientific seriousness by making a joke? But before this matter receives further speculation, it might be well to look for a moment at the birds behind the words.

Six species of grackles sit on the *Quiscalus* branch of the New World blackbirds' family tree (there was a seventh, the slender-billed grackle, now extinct). And of the six, three make themselves at home in the United States. The largest, measuring in at a full foot and a half from bill to tail tip, is *Q. mexicanus*, the great-tailed grackle, and the only member of the trio that never shows itself here at the Point. As the species name indicates, it's a Latino, a bird of the border, thoroughly entrenched along the Mexican frontier from the Gulf to southern California and now expanding its range into Kansas and Colorado. And only the male bird, a polygynous creature, shines glossy black; the slightly smaller female wears brown.

The same his-hers color scheme and the same male penchant for many mates characterize the trio's middle-sized member *Q. major,* the boat-tailed grackle, which is a bird of the Atlantic and Gulf coast marshes. Its tail, however, may be compared to a boat in only one respect, which it shares with other grackle species: In flight the appendage assumes a *V* shape somewhat like that of a keel. I think the tail more truly resembles the long satin train worn by a king in robes of state, except that the bird, walking or at rest, does not drag its feathers on the ground but always holds them beautifully aloft. In autumn, come-and-go flocks of several hundred boat-tails—not mixed blackbirds but boat-tails only—descend on the Point's fields and lawns, where they promenade and peck for food before departing as swiftly as they came. In spring, lone males perch on the topmost branches of riverside pines and most emphatically declare themselves; each ruffles his feathers, flutters his wings so fast that they whistle, and sings an energetic song that sounds just like the twanging of a mouth harp. The third grackle native to the United States is, of course, *Q. quiscula,* the baby of the bunch at a mere foot stem to stern.

And this blackbird, the common grackle, is common indeed. It can hardly be avoided. It ranges across the country from the East Coast to the Rockies and, north to south, from Canadian prairies to the Gulf of Mexico. I see it year-round at my home on the Point— Great Neck Point, a near-wilderness on the banks of North Carolina's wide and salty lower Neuse River. And as the real river moves toward the sea, another kind of blackbird flies into mind—Wallace Stevens's uncommon blackbird, an elegant, sinister darkness set by the poet amid recurrent, pervasively pallid images of snow, ice, and glass. It exists only in the realm of metaphor. Or does it? Release it from the caging stanzas. Use it as an instrument with which to focus on living blackbirds, especially *Q. quiscula.* Behold: In the common grackle's very commonness, in its ubiquity, in its vulgar and over-whelming numbers, its pronounced unpopularity, there suddenly resides an overlooked uncommonness.

There is, for starters, that name. The binomial seems entirely whimsical, a nonce word snatched from thin air or found on the name-giver's doorstep, a foundling bereft of traceable lineage and history. Yet Vieillot was a responsible taxonomist in his dealings with other birds. A Frenchman who spent some years in the States, he not only provided many first-ever descriptions of American birds but gave names to twenty-six genera and thirty-two species. To this day, no small number of Vieillot's designations survive in the ornithological vocabulary: the towhees are still *Pipilo*, the meadowlarks, *Sturnella*, and the vireos, well, *Vireo*. Like most of his names, these three are readily interpreted—"peeper," "little starling," and "greenfinch." But *Quiscalus*? And how could he, who'd surely benefited from a classical education, have chosen to modify that masculine word with a feminine *quiscula*? Did common bird inflame this man with most uncommon inspiration?

All I can find is a supposition, put forth by *The Dictionary of American Birds*, that both little *q* and big *Q* are variants of a single modern Latin word that means "quail." ("Modern" means that it was coined sometime after the end of the Middle Ages.) How peculiar! What connection can possibly exist between a plump, henlike creature and a lean, mean blackbird? Not satisfied, I ask a friend, a renowned classicist, to play detective. Soon thereafter, he reports: "*Quiscalus quiscula*—Scotland Yard is baffled. Read upside down and backwards, the words might be Etruscan perhaps?" Not ready to give up, however, he offers three "wild thoughts," one of which is that the binomial is onomatopoeic, intended to recreate grackle talk rather than qualify as sensible Latin. He wonders, too, if the name-giver might have been thinking of the classical Latin word *quisquiliae*, used by Cicero and others to speak of worthless, rubbishy, throwaway things—and many people, after all, perceive the grackle as the definitively trashy bird. And he even suggests that the binomial might actually be an American Indian bird name fitted out with Latin endings. Now that's a wild thought!

But his efforts don't stop with freewheeling cerebration. He manages to trace the quail definition back to medieval Hungary and Germany. No explanation pops up, though, to explain how a venerable word denoting a European species came to alight on a bird found only in the New World. On with the search. In a Spanish encyclopedia, he finds the entry *Quisqualis*, defined as a genus named by Linnaeus. Aha! Spellings often change with the passing of time, and this word could readily have transformed itself into both of the *Q* words. Nor was it necessarily a name bestowed by

Linnaeus himself; that eminent taxonomist often used names first conceived by others. In this case, might it have been Vieillot? My detective chuckles when he converts this entry in the *Q* collection into English, for it asks the plaintive but pertinent question, "Which of what kind?" It's almost as if the scientists, contemplating grackledom, had scratched their heads, thrown up their hands, and said in grumpy tones, damned if we can figure it out. And then, from France, comes another suggestion. My friend consults *La Grande Larousse*, the Gallic equivalent of *Webster's Unabridged.* To its entry on *quiscale*, the French word for grackle, a note is appended. It cites the opinion of a lexicographer contemporary with Vieillot that the modern Latin scientific term *quiscalus* was probably formed on a word from an American Indian language.

And there the evidence rests, all of it circumstantial, all as muddled as the mind of someone with too many choices. The gracklequail connection does not convince, nor does it seem possible that people who cherish both birds and language would be so careless or so cavalier as to find identity where it cannot exist—unless they were joking or thumbing their scholarly noses. But, oh, I would like to believe that a language now lost but indigenous to America provided an early naturalist with a native name for a native bird. At this late date, however, far from the *Q* words' genesis, we may have to settle for the conundrum—which, and of what kind? As for solving that puzzle, it's likely we'll never make up our minds.

There is, though, one bit of sense, one solace, to be found behind *Quiscalus quiscula*—the bird itself.

III

The common grackles and the red-winged blackbirds descend in their whirling thousands on the stubble of October cornfields just inland from the river. They glean fallen seeds from the earth like black ants polishing the last scraps off a well-picked bone. Grackle bills, so powerful that they can crush acorns, find it easy to break the tough, dry kernels apart.

Overhead, silhouetted against the cloud-frosted sky: the first dark skeins of returning ducks; a great blue heron flying on slow, deliberate wings; the cornfield-scanning appetites of two red-tailed hawks.

IV

Grackle flies above the weedy fields where bright-leaf tobacco once grew. The black wings beat with unfaltering steadiness; the black tail, broader at its pointed tip than at its base, fans wide. The bird's path through the air neither soars nor dips but drives ahead level and straight.

Grackle perches on the lowest limb of a tall loblolly behind the old barn where tobacco was packed. The bird does not always feed on grain and insects. From its bill today's dinner dangles, a five-lined skink, a young one with tail of iridescent blue.

Grackle hops through the newly mowed grass on our lane and regards our approach with wary, glittering attention. Clad only in scraggly, damp-looking pinfeathers, it cannot yet fly. Pushed prematurely from the nest by a sibling? By its own untutored audacity? A parent calling *chuck-chuck-chuck* makes alarmed forays from a nearby pine.

My husband and I observe these events. As we watch, we fly and hop, we perch and feed ourselves. We cry out to our reckless young. We fear for our lives.

V

Tssh-kleet!
Koguba-leek!
These are alphabetically encoded simulations of the common grackle's song as found in two widely used field guides. These are also the ingenious cries of human bafflement and desperation. But how else might the grackle's inflections be hinted at?

Perhaps by augmenting invented syllables with audible pictures:

the screak of chalk on a blackboard, the haunted creaking of an unoiled hinge.

As I play with descriptions of the grackle's voice, outside in the yard a grackle sings, describing itself. But, artifice and nature, both have their place. I do not know which I prefer, the truth of the original or the truth of homage, bird song grating dissonant or the suggestive silence of print.

VI

For centuries people have shivered in the swarming darkness thrown by grackles over planted fields.

Of grackles and their close cousins the red-winged blackbirds, John Lawson, Surveyor General for the Lords Proprietors of the Carolinas, said in 1709 that they "are the worst Vermine in America. They fly sometimes in such Flocks, that they destroy everything before them."

About thirty years later, describing this same species, which he calls the purple jack daw, the British naturalist Mark Catesby wrote: "They make their nests on the branches of trees in all parts of the country, but most in remote and unfrequented places; from whence in autumn, after a vast increase, they assemble together, and come amongst the inhabitants in such numbers that they sometimes darken the air, and are seen in continued flights for miles together, making great devastation of grain where they light. In winter they flock to barn doors. They have a rank smell; their flesh is coarse, black, and is seldom eaten."

Nearly a century after that, John James Audubon depicted a pair of grackles: The male, head thrown back as if in triumph, clings to a shredded, pulled-back piece of corn husk; perched on an untouched ear above him, his mate seems to eye him with full approbation. And Audubon made comment on this drawing: "Look at them. The male, as if full of delight at the sight of the havoc which he has already committed on the tender, juicy, unripe corn on which he stands, has swelled his throat, and is calling in exultation to his companions to come and assist him in demolishing it. The female has fed herself, and is about to fly off with a well-loaded bill to her hungry and expectant brood. See how the husk is torn from the ear, and how nearly devoured are the grains of corn!"

And today, particularly in the southeastern states, swarms that may number as many as a million birds still materialize from who knows where to savage crops of corn, rice, and other grains. Nor are they easily scared off, but at their own black leisure fill up hollow craws before they rise and fly away.

At such times, now and then and in years to come, it is as if the idea of malevolence has cast a million living, working, all-consuming shadows.

VII

Truly, the learned nomenclators imagined golden birds. And truly, those in charge of scientific names regarded the blackbirds with a jaundiced eye when they chose *Icteridae* as the formal name for the New World family that includes orioles, meadowlarks, cowbirds, grackles, and quite a few others. The name comes from the Greek word *ikteros*, which means "jaundice" and was also used to refer to a handsome European bird that's not an Icterid at all but a member of another family, the Oriolidae. That bird, not related to American birds with the same common name, is the golden oriole, *Oriolus oriolus*, with bright yellow body and sooty wings. (According to Pliny, the Roman natural historian, this bird and the ailment were linked by more than the sharing of a name and a color: Someone suffering from jaundice would be cured simply by glancing at a golden oriole. But the bird, alas, did not take kindly to such treatment, and it would die.) The word *oriole* itself is a word that holds far more than a hint of yellow; it comes from a fond diminutive for *aureus*, the Latin word meaning "golden."

Oriole and Icterid, it's not strictly an accident of nomenclatorial imagination that variations on the theme of yellow play throughout the names of the New World blackbirds. Many of them are showy creatures. Male orioles of many species wear fine plumage that is spun of rust or leaping flames; the females are no less handsome in feathers that range in color from richest gold to delicate chartreuse. Meadowlarks of both sexes gleam with gold at throat and chest. Male bobolinks in breeding dress are decked with pale gold caps. And some of the species bearing *blackbird* as an official part of their common names also flaunt or hide bright colors—the bold and brassy yellow-headed blackbird, the more modest red-winged blackbird that displays crimson epaulets with golden fringe in flight but often hides them when it's perched.

But grackles, the blackest of blackbirds, must settle for iridescence, a sheen of purple or bronze that floats on their feathers like oil on dark water. On sunless days, the sheen winks out. Even the grackles' common name removes them from the realm of golden birds. Coming from *gracula*, Latin for jackdaw, it puts them in the swart and lightless company of crows.

If, however, the grackles have been scanted, their jaunty, creaking darkness given short shrift, responsibility for such neglect does not lie solely with the nomenclators. The givers of names, like the rest of us, have shown an all too human preference for precious metal over smudgy coal, for sunlight's dazzle over subterranean night.

VIII

I know that the blackbird is involved in what I know. It's been involved as long as I can remember, even longer. And many Americans know it: the blackbird found in the noble company of kings and queens, the bird couched in the clear and cradling rhythms of Mother Goose. Listen!

> Sing a song of sixpence,
> Pockets full of rye,
> Four and twenty blackbirds
> Baked in a pie,
> And when the pie was opened,
> The birds began to sing.
> Now wasn't that a dainty dish
> To set before the king!

An astonishing dish! In a mere few lines a miracle takes place. Though the fate of the twenty-four birds may gag the sensibilities of anyone not accustomed to the idea of cooking and eating little wild birds, it is totally canceled by the song that bursts with great good cheer from the opened pie: out of death, a melodious resurrection.

The blackbird is further involved in what we know. Listen again:

> The king was in his counting house
> Counting out his money.
> The queen was in the parlor
> Eating bread and honey.
> The maid was in the garden
> Hanging out the clothes,
> And along came a blackbird
> That snipped off her nose!

And the fingers of the grown-up chanting the verse fly toward the child-listener's nose and give it a tweak. Oh look! The grown-up holds a nose—a *nose*, mind you, not a thumb—between index and middle fingers. But as quickly as it was snipped off, the nose is put back in its natural place. Child squeals with delight and asks for an instant rerun of verse and game.

As child and as parent of children, I have known this blackbird forever. But what I have not known until recently is that the blackbird involved in this part of what I know is not any blackbird that I have ever seen. The grackles do not, in the usual course of grackle events, have the chance to set their large, bright eyes on a king or a queen, nor do any of the Icterids that boast the word *blackbird* as part of their standard English names. Every last one of the nearly one hundred members of the blackbird family is a bird of the Americas. But Mother Goose's blackbird—and venerable Mother G. herself—are denizens of Britain. And her blackbird is really a thrush, *Turdus merula*, the European counterpart of the American robin, *T. migratorius*. Except for the colors of their plumage (and the presence or absence of royalty in the immediate environment), our robin and the bird of nursery rhyme are so alike that size and posture, habits and habitat, make no nevermind. To get a mind's-eye glimpse of the birds that snip off noses and sing from opened pies, imagine the familiar robin but dress the female in dark brown and, for the male, retain our robin's yellow bill but color the feathers grackle black.

I know now that British blackbirds have always been involved in what I know. I know, too, that the grackle is like them because it obeys the same inescapable avian rhythms that take their measures from the rise and fall of on-rolling seasons. And I know that the grackle is also utterly unlike Mother Goose's blackbirds: It sings its own grating, screaking song. Indeed, like a poet manqué, it sings and celebrates itself—but otherwise remains unsung.

What does the real blackbird know? What, the grackle? I do not, cannot, shall never know. But it seems most unlikely that I am in any way involved in what *they* know.

IX

No grackle, not one, in sight. The air is empty, as are the pine-branch perches and the strutting sand along the river. But on a patch of grass still early-morning shaded from the sun of May, a grackle has left half of an eggshell. Its greeny-blue paleness is inscribed with purple scrawls as bold as graffiti. The message, however, is delivered by the shell itself: Out of endings, beginnings—the edge of one circle touches the next.

Circles within circles: The eggs have been cupped in a loosely woven round of twigs and tough, dry stems lined with slightly finer stuff. Though she is one of a monogamous pair, the female bird has obeyed the mandates for her species and alone constructed the nest, alone incubated the eggs. But her mate stayed close, keeping her under his jealous eye. And when the eggs cracked open and split, releasing their gawping contents, they both took the fragments of shell one by one in their long black bills and flew them out of sight lest eggshell clutter on the ground below the nest alert a predator to the helpless morsels newly hatched above. To keep the nest clean, the pair will also dispose of the hatchlings' tidily encapsulated feces by carrying off or consuming them. Nor will the tasks of the adult birds end with the fledging of their young; newly feathered, stump-tailed offspring, scattered in the nearby shrubbery, shall call out with strident insistence for continued care. They'll keep their parents hopping for a week, keep them in the air, keep them at the shifting epicenter of a greedy, giddy, clamorous whirl. Then, tails grown long, they will fly apart, spun off and away in the giant centrifuge of the search for self-sufficiency. Their flights will mark the edges of many new circles.

Shell on the grass, no grackle in sight: Spring to spring, the year has come round, and the grackle, too, has circled around, meeting itself.

X

Over the April rivers of greening leaves and grass, the grackles spill themselves like a million million drops of oil. In search of food, the flocks seep thickly, silently over fields and lawns. Or they alight in the treetops to spread their songs in creaky, ever-widening ripples on the air. Sharp sounds—a slamming door, a shout, a clap of hands—may whisk the screeching multitude upward and away. Or may not. The grackles listen to the season's music and find their rhythms in the beating reproductive pulse.

XI

Usually, I sit within the walls of my own cozy skin and look at the rest of the world through the window of self-interest. But sometimes outside events loom so large that they call for another kind of attention: autumnal grackles gathering wing to colonial wing in their primeval fashion and settling by the hundreds of thousands to roost in the piney woods that border the soy and corn fields just inland from the river. Their raucous voices abrade the cold air. Their black feathers absorb all light. Without the least awareness or intent, they force me to recognize their absolute and invincible otherness.

The grackles exist. I exist. They do not acknowledge me, nor can

I hope to cure them of being themselves. But for a moment it is not impossible for me to emerge from the shadows of my own self-concern.

XII

The river Neuse is moving. It has welled from its upland source and moved toward the sea for two million years.

The grackle is flying upriver and down. For two million years, it has flown as it pleases, drawing its swift, dark, disappearing, reappearing line above the water's glass calms and white-capped turbulence.

The grackle's ancestor, the parent of all Icterids, flew as it pleased a dozen million years or more before there was a river Neuse.

XIII

All afternoon, flocks of grackles spread their creaking darkness over fields and woods. In swirling black drifts, they are gathering and going to gather. I stand in the yard watching, leaning against a loblolly pine.

The Lives of the Pelican

Thirty-two brown pelicans fly over the river Neuse in a straight, steady, follow-the-leader line. With choral precision, they fly just inches over the salty water, wings beating, beating firmly, pausing to hold for a long smooth glide, then beating again. The flight is large, another of the many big ones we've seen this winter. And it would be even larger if we were to count the invisible pelicans—shadow birds, alter egos, doppelflieger—that flap and glide and plunge for fish along with the visible thirty-two.

A good many birds lead double lives, one as a real bird tending to its own avian affairs, the other as the feathered, flying embodiment of some human idea. A dove is a dove is a symbol of peace. An eagle is itself and at the same time has been appropriated for its fierce, wild majesty to serve as the emblem of a nation. The vulture is not merely an efficient undertaker but a dark-robed fortune-teller predicting death before it occurs. Crows and owls may also bode ill, and ravens, as everybody knows, now and forevermore shall croak negative comments. To counter such gloom, let bluebirds bring in the happiness for which they're famed. Let robins always represent spring. And some kinds of birds go even farther; they don't stop simply at giving tangible form to ideas and feelings but offer continuing, reproductive proof of mythical times—the kingfisher that was a queen, the osprey and woodpeckers that were and ever shall be kings. Between most birds and what they're thought to represent, there's some benign congruity at work.

But not for the pelican. Though the bird I see flying over North Carolina's river Neuse, the bird selected by Louisiana as its official mascot, behaves as it was impeccably programmed to do some thirty to forty million years ago, it's haunted by a host of shadow birds. The trouble is, people can't seem to agree about the pelican. Is it a risible Rube Goldberg contraption, a patchwork assemblage of unlikely parts that just happens to catch fish? Or is its awkward-looking construction really a modest, Lincolnesque disguise for shining excellence and inward beauty?

But before I go into the shadow birds, will the real pelican fly past, making a token appearance? With rare unanimity (but slightly different spellings), both Greeks and Romans used the same word, calling the bird *Pelecanus*, which is still the sole genus name for the world's seven species. All seven species have the famous extensible pouch of skin at the junction of jaw and throat; it is catchment and sieve, retaining fish but letting water out. Two of the seven species are born and bred in North America: *P. erythrorhynchus*, "tawny-red bill" or the American white pelican, and *P. occidentalis*, "pelican of the west" or the brown pelican. All but one species prefer fresh inland waters, and all but one swim after their finny prey, herding fish and scooping them up in dip-net bills. The oddball, of course, is the bird of the golden west. The brown pelican is an old salt and a daredevil diver. It may take a young bird at least one full, most perilous year to become adept at hurtling down headfirst to take a fish. Hesitant beginners paddle on the surface and imitate the less audacious freshwater pelicans by using their pouches as scoops to catch whatever swims below. With bodies more than a yard long and wings that may spread at full stretch to seven feet, brown pelicans are not dainty birds. Attaining lift-off from the water calls for a gawky, slapdash run on super-sized webbed feet. And almost invariably the wings of brown pelicans look tatty because they never seem to sport a full complement of flight feathers. At three or four years, the birds mature and breed in crowded colonies. At any age, they're social creatures. Curling their long necks back so that chests may give support to huge bills, grown birds and juveniles fly together in long flap-glide formations or break for bouts of plunge-diving when the fish are schooling. Young and old, the pelicans capture their food in those wonderful bills. . . .

Enter the first alter ego, the figure made comedic by one feature so attention-riveting that it renders every other feature inconspicuous—the nose of Cyrano de Bergerac, the speech impediment of Elmer Fudd. Here is the pelican as super-pouch, the prodigy much commented on by ancient observers, including Pliny. He tells us that "Pelicans look rather like swans and would not really differ from swans except"—here comes the punch line—"that they have a second stomach in their throats." Pliny goes on to relate that as a pelican eats, the insatiable bird stores every morsel in its throat pouch, and only when the pouch is crammed till it can hold no more does the bird at last return the food to its mouth and then, like some ruminant animal, pass it along to the true stomach. The truth, of course, is one stomach per pelican, nor does the bird use the contents of its pouch as a cud.

Since Pliny, super-pouch is the pelican most frequently given a nod of recognition. One such acknowledgment comes from John Lawson, the Englishman who catalogued wildlife along the Carolina coast in 1709. The brown pelican—he calls it "Pellican of the Wilderness"—receives only cursory mention, and the reason for such short shrift is that the bird, unlike most on his list, is not in any way considered fit to eat. But according to Lawson, it does, yes it does, have one use: The skin of its throat can be turned into a tobacco pouch.

Much more recently, in what might be called the juvenile years of the twentieth century, super-pouch soared to ridiculous heights and dived into a limerick. I used to blame Ogden Nash for this state of affairs but have lately discovered the culprit to be one Dixon Lanier Merritt. His lines are so exuberantly silly that they bear repeating:

A wonderful bird is the pelican,
His bill will hold more than his belican.
He can take in his beak
Food enough for a week,
But I'm damned if I see how the helican.

Count on Edward Lear, he of "The Owl and the Pussycat," to continue the fun. Seeing the whole bird rather than just its amazing bill, he presents the pelican pleased with itself. Though the species to which he refers is not one of the American duo, all the pelicans are social birds, and the river might well be the Neuse with its sandbars, instead of the Nile.

We live on the Nile. The Nile we love.
By night we sleep on the cliffs above.
By day we fish, and at eve we stand
On long bare islets of yellow sand.

Ploffskin, Pluffskin, Pelican jee!
We think no birds so happy as we!
Plumpskin, Plashkin, Pelican jill!
We think so then, and we thought so still.

—"The Pelican Chorus"

But not all of the pelican's doppelflieger are so merry. Lawson's "pellican," for all that its pouch may be used to carry tobacco, is one of a far less giddy, far more somber pair of shadow birds than those of Pliny, Merritt, and Lear. Lawson takes his phrase from the Prayer Book of 1622: "I am become like a pelican in the wilderness: and like an owl that is in the desert." This is the pelican as symbol, standing in for human isolation, helplessness, and hope.

The other of the pair is the pelican as paradigm, the bird that Shakespeare lauds as "the kind life-rend'ring pelican." He refers to a fable that must be as old as the flood, as old as the first human sight of pelicans. It seems that the adult bird, wielding its great bill as a sword, pierces its own breast so that its nestlings may receive the right red nourishment. Such piety and devotion, such self-sacrifice in the exercise of parental duty, made the bird so admirable, so glorious, that it was installed in the Middle Ages' aviary of heraldic birds. A belief that the pelican does indeed feed its young on its own blood has somehow seeped from the long-ago past into the twentieth century; one reputable encyclopedia cautions readers not to credit such a tale.

The next shadow bird bears a fairly close resemblance to the bird that casts the shadow. If only it could be literally seen and touched, it might be taken for the real bird—or, more precisely, for four birds, a quartet of wild brown pelicans. These are the once and future pelicans, which have been given a literary exemption from finitude in lines by the American poet Robinson Jeffers (1887–1962). He accurately notes the typical raggedness of the birds' flight feathers and in a splendid twist converts the birds' awkward and almost archaic appearance into a warranty of power:

> Four pelicans went over the house,
> Sculled their worn oars over the courtyard: I saw that
>   ungainliness
> Magnifies the idea of strength.

Amid wheeling gulls, the four birds fly and are seen by the poet as living connections with life and events in earlier epochs—the seeding of the first redwood, the soaring of pterodactyl and archaeopteryx, Pangaia breaking into continents. For Jeffers, pelicans fuse an unimaginable antiquity with the present moment, and they are evidence that "Nothing at all has suffered erasure. There is a life not of our time."

Or, as Edward Lear more lightly puts it: "We think so then, and we thought so still." The past is, the present shall be, and the future was.

*   *   *

Shadow bird after shadow bird, but none comes close to indicating the true miracle. Will the real *P. occidentalis* please fly by again? Yes? Thank you! Here on the river, the day's total exceeds three hundred birds. We've counted only the morning commuters heading upriver, where many of them spend the day perched wing to wing, body to jostling body on the jutting piers of nearby Clubfoot Creek. Because the evening traffic downriver will include many of these same birds, we do not count them. Nor do we need to consider their shadows. Brown pelicans, the real ones, are quite enough. And by themselves are more astounding, more miraculous than any of the simulacra hatched by human fancy.

Five years ago, the river—indeed, the whole southeastern coast of the United States—was almost bereft of pelicans. Here, not far from Pamlico Sound, we might see one or two during an entire year, usually a lost-looking juvenile perched to nap or preen amid the gulls on a sandbar. The species almost suffered erasure. The reproductive chemistry of pelicans, like that of osprey, eagles, and many others, was so affected by chemicals of the DDT sort that their eggs were too thin-shelled for viability. After DDT was banned, the numbers of osprey rebounded quickly. The pelicans, however, have taken their own sweet, ungainly time. But now they fish and fly over the river in numbers great enough to show that they have a brand-new lease on a life that's very much of our time.

A Bird of Tradition

Canvasbacks! The first week in January 1990 is one for the bird-watching record books. Daylong, flocks of a hundred or more paddle back and forth not thirty feet off our bulkhead. They feed busily, diving beneath the sun-shot water, surfacing, diving under again. Sometimes, they rush into flight but turn and settle back, or are replaced by another mob. Mornings and evenings, the numbers of canvasbacks are even greater—not flights in the relatively trifling hundreds but in the thousands, tens of thousands, winging in great, swift, steady V's upriver and down. The Chief and I have never before seen so many cans off Great Neck Point, and many of the neighbors, people who've been here far longer than we, are equally amazed. It's the custom of these birds to winter farther north, in Chesapeake Bay or North Carolina's Currituck Sound. Under normal circumstances, we often spot small groups of ten or so birds bobbing five hundred yards out amid larger gatherings of other ducks. But at 1990's advent, circumstances are far from ordinary. It is as if every last can on the Atlantic coast has mustered just off our front yard.

Nor have we seen such an assemblage of other ducks at one time. As usual, the scaup are rafted a hundred yards offshore, and buffleheads ply the river in small groups—nothing new here. Nor is there anything extraordinary about the dozen clannish black scoter that utter low, tremulous whistles as they ride the water at several wing-lengths from the thronging scaup. But the rest! Ring-necked ducks cruise in close proximity to the scaup. Ring-necks? Their collars of dark chestnut feathers are well nigh invisible. They should have been called ring-bills for the highly noticeable bands of white that encircle both male and female bills near the tip. Amid these ring-billed ring-necks, other river-loving ducks bob on the steel-grey water—red-breasted mergansers, a few redheads. And marsh ducks hang like satellites on the fringes of the crowd—wigeon, gadwall, the small hooded mergansers, a lone female wood duck. The assortment surprises, for dabblers such as these prefer the marsh-defended seclusion of the pond's landward end. Nor are the ducks the only waterfowl in sight. Three coots swim briskly on the short stretch of river between our bulkhead and the creek. If not for the give-away white of their bills, they'd be seen only as charcoal-grey shadows moving rapidly across the water. Just yards upstream from the coots, on the sandbar where creek spills into the river, still more ducks have congregated. Big black ducks waddle at water's edge on blaze-orange legs, and mallards hunker down to preen—wild mallards, not the half-tame, home-raised beggars that work this waterfront year-round.

Ducks and more ducks! Canvasbacks by hundreds and thousands! The question is, why? What on earth has possessed them all to come *here*? Weather even more amazing than the feathered multitude suggests an answer. If this first week of 1990 is one for the bird-watching books, Christmas of 1989 was one for the annals of coastal meteorology.

The day of Christmas Eve, the temperatures plummeted along the Carolina coast, and snow began to fall. It fell through Christmas Day. And on the twenty-seventh, when we left winter quarters in Virginia and returned to the river for a post-holiday rest, we arrived in an unknown country.

Snow lay twelve cold inches deep on lawns and fields. It piled in four-foot drifts along the windward sides of the hedgerows and lifted in long, gauzy plumes on the frigid breath of a northeast wind. Icicles hung heavy from eaves and piers; pier pilings were swaddled in thick wrappings of yellowish ice and wore bulky turbans of frozen spray. And the river, the wide salty river, looked strangely flat and calm—no whitecaps, no waves, not even a ripple. Shore to distant shore, the usually restless surface was frozen into quietude—five miles of sunlight scattered into tiny, brilliant fragments, five miles of solid, diamantine ice. According to the records, the last such freeze occurred in 1926. Oh what an improbable celebration, what a once-in-a-lifetime display the elements created to usher in the twentieth century's last decade!

Though the near-arctic cold had stilled all the apparent motion of the river itself, the glittering plain of its surface supported all manner of noise, activity, life. Squawking gulls, the ring-bills, and the great black-backs flocked on the ice as they would on a summer sandbar. Two great blue herons, one near the creek upriver, the other off our bulkhead, lifted their legs high, as if they were wading through water, not air, as they hunted for their dinners. The near bird lunged, struck with its long bill, and bounced back. The minnows in the wintry river tantalized, but they were out of reach, embedded just below the topmost layer of the ice. The local pack of black Labs romped vociferously offshore, one yelping in surprise when he skidded on a slick patch. People were out there too, discovering that, given the proper miracle, they really could walk on water.

Fifty yards offshore, teenaged K. D. performed this astonishing feat. Bundled against the cold, lugging a five-gallon bucket, she moved upriver at the slow, deliberate pace of the herons. Like the herons, she kept her gaze downward, closely inspecting the ice and all it contained. I was reminded of the summer treasure hunts that frequently take place at river's edge or in the water itself—searches for Indian artifacts, ballast stones from the old sailing ships, antique soda bottles, lumber from piers demolished by hard storms. But in such bright and glittering cold, what could K. D. have been looking for? Oh. She took a hatchet from her bucket and began to chop. The stout hatchet proved far more effective than a heron's slender bill. Five minutes later, using her mittened hands as pry bars, she'd extracted a fish, a very large fish, from the ice. It turned out to be a spotted sea trout. Three days before, that trout had been swimming, feeding, minding its own finny business. Then, the sudden on-slaught of near-zero temperatures caught it in a trap of ice, and the trap had sprung shut so swiftly that the fish was still as fresh as any that had been netted, cleaned, and stowed last summer in the shed's fifteen-cube freezer within an hour of being taken from the water. It turned out, too, that K. D. had known what she was looking for. An earlier stroll atop the river had shown her the bounty beneath. What a fine trout! Its silvery body, speckled with black polka dots on upper sides and dorsal fin, shone in the sunlight. Its name, of course, was Feast.

Gulls and herons, black Labs, girl out fishing with a hatchet, but not a duck in sight. But as it happened, the trout was taken from the river's deep freeze in the nick of time. The next day, the temperature began to rise. The earth's snow cover shrank rapidly in the warming air; on the windswept portions of lawns and fields, bare patches appeared, attracting hordes of juncos, sparrows, bluebirds, and meadowlarks that searched so hungrily for seeds and grubs they did not fly up in alarm when people walked past. The river still gleamed in unaccustomed stasis, but at the creek, the ice broke apart and narrow leads of water opened up. The first to find these feeding holes were the big dabble ducks, the blacks and the mal-lards, that packed the leads of open water wing to wing, or rump to rump as they stood on their heads, tails in the air, to look under-water for food.

The next day, and the next, the temperature continued to climb. The ice on the river creaked and drifted away from shore; loosening its grip, the ice on piers and pilings splashed into the water. The scaup came, and the tiny buffleheads, the mergansers, scoter, and ring-billed ring-necks. Hey, gang, the party's at Great Neck Point— plenty of rafting room, lots of good eats. By New Year's Day, the canvasbacks in their prodigious thousands outnumbered all the rest.

The cans on the winter river have traveled a mighty distance from their summer breeding grounds. Some may have nested and reared their young in the arctic and subarctic regions of the far northwest— the MacKenzie River delta in Canada's Northwest Territories, the flats of the Yukon River in Alaska. Some will have nested somewhat farther to the south at the edge of marshy lakes in the boreal forest region or in the prairie wetlands of Canada's central provinces. Still others may have arrived on the river from summer territory within the United States, the pothole country found in the northernmost states of the Midwest. At summer's end, after the young have fledged, canvasbacks migrate down every flyway in North America on their southward journey. Though some seek balmier climates such as that of central Mexico, most are headed for one of two major wintering grounds, either the mid-Atlantic coast or, a continent away, the coast of California. They dally en route before they settle in by October's end, but they could probably set speed records if they were ever so inclined. Cans are large ducks, as heavy as mallards or blacks but faster in flight: Their speed has been clocked at seventy miles per hour. As early as February, they may leave to fly north, taking wing long before the ice in their summering grounds has broken up.

How handsome these high-fliers are—the females dignified in shades of light grey and a warm rusty brown; the slightly bigger males with sleek auburn heads, black chests, white bellies, and backs covered not by canvas but a fine weave of palest grey linen. Their profiles are almost Greek, foreheads descending in an unbroken slope to the tips of the long, dark grey bills.

This elegance is imperiled. Of all the widely distributed game ducks in America, they are the least numerous. And the species has been in trouble for a long time. No single factor carries the blame; the reasons are many and varied. Some of their difficulties—not all, but some—may be directly attributed to the negative impacts of humankind not only on habitat but on the birds themselves. In the earlier decades of this century, their numbers were certainly decimated by the market gunners who shot them (and many other birds) to appease almost quenchless appetites for food and fashion—the meat for the table and the feathers for m'lady's hat. The cans may have suffered more than most: Research has uncovered the mournful fact that female canvasbacks, especially in the first two years of life, fall victim more readily than hens of other species to thumping guns. Why? The reason may be nothing more than an instinctual unwariness that posed no survival disadvantage until this century. Then, decades' worth of drainage projects to convert prairie marshes to arable farmland have robbed the cans of former nesting sites. Recurrent, wholly natural droughts have compounded these losses. Sometimes, of course, drought's opposite may bring prolonged rains that flood and drown shore-hugging nests, but the creeping desiccation of marshy land is the more usual process. Predators are not to be discounted either. Skunks, crows, ravens, and magpies have always favored succulent eggs, and in just the last forty years another egg lover, the raccoon, has steadily worked its way into far northern regions—canvasback regions—in which it had previously been unknown. A threat is also posed by another species of duck, the redhead, which sometimes behaves like a cowbird, laying its eggs in a canvasback's nest and casually departing to leave their care to somebody else. The upshot is often that, refusing to brood the eggs of a parasitic intruder, the nest's true proprietor ignores her own clutch, and the next generation dies *in ovo*. Under all these pressures, the population of canvasbacks has declined as if it were rolling with gathering speed down a steep, downhill slope, despite federal and state efforts that were initiated as long ago as 1936 to protect the species from shooters' guns. But laws cannot be written to stem the destructive work of raccoons, redheads, and adverse weather.

And no legislation can ever undo genetically programmed stubbornness. "The canvasback is a bird of tradition," says Charles S. Potter, Jr., Executive Vice President of the North American Wildlife Foundation. Through its Delta Waterfowl and Wetlands Research Station in central Manitoba, prime canvasback country, the NAWF has monitored the species for more than half a century, since 1938.

Among its discoveries is the troublesome fact that a female canvasback will breed only in the area in which she herself was hatched and fledged. No substitutes are acceptable. If for some reason she cannot go home, or goes home to find that her natal wetlands have succumbed to drought or the plow, she will not breed that year. Instead, she'll hold back on reproduction and wait for a year with favorably moist conditions—a year that may never come. When she and her barren sisters die, their breeding tradition dies with them. And never again, not even if former wetlands are restored or the rains fall torrential, is it likely that the canvasback, a bird that neither adapts nor pushes beyond old, familiar, programmed limits, will ever nest in that area again: once forgotten, forgotten forever.

Yet during the phenomenal January of 1990, thousands on thousands of canvasbacks wing over the cold, grey river and touch down with swirling commotions to raft and feed. Speculation says that they are here because the waters just a hundred miles to the north are still locked in an icy fist. Many of the other species present are also frozen out of their usual feeding grounds—the dabble ducks, for example, have been pushed out into the river because ice remains thick on their pond. The river offers an open surface on which all may raft, dabblers and divers alike, and illustrate their very duckness by ducking under time and again to find the victuals they need to survive the winter and make their journeys north come milder weather.

The word *duck* comes from *dūcan*, an Old English verb meaning "to dive." And the canvasbacks' scientific name, *Aythya valisineria*, refers directly to the favorite tidbit for which the species dives. Given a choice, cans duck with relish into subaqueous meadows of *Vallisneria spiralis*, wild celery, a plant with long, curling leaves that grows in brackish water. (*Valisineria*, the spelling found in the species designation, is a nonesuch word and proves only that a taxonomist may be excellent at observation but poor at orthography.) Cans are herbivores at heart, also grazing on such plants as eelgrass, wigeon grass, and sago pondweed. Some of the meadows lie deep, but cans are able to dive down as far as thirty feet in search of their suppers. Imagine, a three-pound duck at thirty feet! But the bird is not completely picky and will indeed indulge in meat—midges, the larvae of caddis and mayflies, snails, shrimp, the eggs of spawning fish. And it's meat that they're after in the shallow waters off our front yard; at this point in its long course, the river does not offer greens worth speaking of.

From too many sources, the cans are under threat of diminishment, of dwindling away to nothing but a memory. But the astonishing multitude of January 1990 seems to encourage hope. Frank C. Bellrose says in his authoritative guide *Ducks, Geese, and Swans of North America*, "For most species of ducks, breeding ground data are considered the better indices of yearly change in abundance, but the January inventory figures are deemed the more valid for canvasbacks." He does not give a reason. But with such a huge New Year's concentration of cans on one tiny stretch of river, might not some hope be justified?

Hope springs also from other sources. Very little can be done to hold back natural adversaries, but efforts have certainly been launched to curtail human depredations, to slow the incursions of farming into the wild marshes and, in some cases, to reverse the process. Such efforts range from the grand to the informal. On the one hand, organizations such as Ducks Unlimited and The Nature Conservancy make relatively large-scale acquisitions of habitat suitable for nesting; on the other, there's the enterprising, individualized Adopt a Pothole Program cooperatively sponsored by the Louisiana Outdoor Writers Association and the NAWF. The Adopt a Pothole Program zeroes in on privately owned potholes, those low-lying, prairie-country wetlands in which many kinds of ducks have immemorially summered and reproduced. For each acre taken under a protective wing, the adopter antes up a yearly contribution of one hundred dollars, which is used to compensate a farmer for holding his land back from drainage and cultivation and, thus, maintaining its allure for ducks. Adopt a Pothole, however, is more likely to benefit species of waterfowl other than the canvasback, for the bird of tradition must breed on home grounds or not breed at all.

On most of their wintering grounds, the canvasbacks have ceased to be fair game for hunters. Hunting regulations attempt to protect the birds and to stimulate an increase in their numbers by declaring the season on the species closed until further notice. Only if their populations rebound will the season be reopened and canvasbacks once again be considered legitimate targets. Protection is also offered not just to cans but to all waterfowl by a joint venture of the United States and Canada. In 1986, the two countries approved the North American Waterfowl Management Plan, which is intended to restore the many, sadly dwindling populations of ducks, geese, and swans by saving and improving both summer and winter habitat. The plan has identified geographic areas worth attention and has designated the more important as "high priority waterfowl focus areas." One of these is the lower Neuse and its marshes.

The river in my front yard, the bays and sounds immediately to our north, the far-away prairies, the boreal forests, the arctic rivers flowing through tundra—it's hard to imagine any of these without their canvasbacks. The odds, however, do not seem to favor the bird. It's a likely candidate for joining the dodo and the passenger pigeon in never-never land. But in the winter of 1990, the cans on the river enjoyed a month of grace.

But they didn't. They still don't, not on this river at any rate. Nor, by extension, are the cans and their kin safe in many other wintering areas.

"Dilution is the solution to pollution!"

So goes the war cry of North Carolina's environmental managers. We first hear it in March 1990, weeks after the canvasbacks have left the river and started their trans-American flights to the breeding grounds. For us, the cry begins as a printed whisper, a half-inch announcement in the local newspaper's public notices section. It tells us that the state will issue a wastewater permit, effective April 30, to the Marine Corps Air Station at Cherry Point. The permit allows construction of a new outfall to replace one in present use. But, unlike the one in present use, it will discharge treated wastes directly into the lower Neuse. The tiny notice, best read with a magnifying glass, is counterpointed by front-page features trumpeting the results of a new study conducted by geologist Stanley Riggs of East Carolina University. The study shows excessively high concentrations of heavy metals—lead, mercury, and cadmium among them—on the riverbed beneath other direct outfalls. Cherry Point repairs aircraft: paints, acids, metals. These by-products of the repair process are currently treated and deposited, along with other wastes, in a tributary creek, which has served unintentionally as a settling pond because the shallow creek mouth acts as a dam to keep sludge from entering the river. (Swimming and other recreations, like father-son fishing contests, still take place in the creek, though signs warn of hazards to human health.) Allowing such stuff to be dumped in the Neuse—what can the bureaucrats be thinking of? And it's the administrators of the state's Division of Environmental Management—not its conscientious men in the field, not the Marines, but the DEM's administrators—who make the decisions here for better or worse. The military has simply applied for a permit and, when it's issued, must obey the terms approved by the DEM; the military is guilty only of taking the path of least resistance (and lowest cost) rather than working with—pushing and shoving—the DEM to find ways of keeping our waters clean.

What's going on? How is it that the public guardians of environmental health and safety can act to the detriment of the river and all the life it supports—and not just marine and bird life but that of the people on its banks? The Point and other riverside communities are all abuzz. Poking around, sampling opinions, asking questions, we investigate. And what we find is the local version of a larger story that encompasses all the country's rivers and lakes, bays and estuaries.

From its headwaters northwest of Raleigh to its meeting with the sea in Pamlico Sound, the Neuse flows 315 miles. Along its course, 317 outfalls dump municipal and industrial effluents straight into the water, and this figure does not include outfalls like the one at Cherry Point that discharge into tributary creeks rather than into the river itself. Nor are these wastes always adequately treated; sometimes, with unplanned-for overloads, they're not treated at all. To such discharges, the sources of which can be pinpointed, add the liquid trash from nonpoint sources, among them the myriad individual septic systems of unincorporated riverside communities like Great Neck Point and the drainage ditches that crosshatch the land and carry away everything—agricultural chemicals, parking-lot oil slicks—that is swept up by the runoff from heavy rains. The rationale behind the dilution theory is, of course, that the river is large enough and swift enough to cleanse itself of insults, most especially in the lower Neuse, twenty-odd miles long and five astounding miles wide.

The size of the newly proposed insult is equally astounding: three and a half million gallons per day of mixed domestic and industrial sewage. No matter that the models for the new outfall, based on the fresh water of the river's upper reaches, ignore the lower river's salinity. No matter that the meeting of salt water with fresh sets up a density-driven pattern of water circulation that causes the river's bottom currents to flow vigorously *up*stream. No matter that the model makers, plugging nonexistent astronomical tides into their calculations, have scanted the fact that the river's vertical movements, its rise and fall, are governed by wind tides—wind from the south, the water runs low and relatively sweet; wind from the north, it rises, pushed in from salty Pamlico Sound. And no matter that the permit approves relaxed standards for most of the components of the discharge, including the heavy metals. After all, the river is big enough to take care of itself. But three river-hugging counties rally to protest the permit's issuance. The DEM scratches April 30 as the permit's effective date and schedules a public hearing for Thursday, May 17.

And on the critical evening, the hearing room is packed, standing room only. Citizen after citizen rises to make factual and remarkably dispassionate comment in the three-minute span allotted each speaker. A commercial crabber says that his catch in the last few years has shown a rising incidence of crabshell disease, an erosive ailment that's probably triggered, according to marine biologists, by a decline in water quality. A fisherman also cites degradation of the waters and shows charts that illustrate a nosedive during the last decade in the number of finfish taken from the river. A water-skier makes the point that the new outfall would be located uncomfortably close to a public beach. Our neighbor Mo, a retired helicopter mechanic who owes his pension to Cherry Point, states flatly that such an outfall would automatically shove the area's water-quality classification into a lower category, a change quite specifically forbidden by the Clean Water Act. A geologist questions the adequacy of modeling the permit on freshwater conditions. An oncologist, who works with children suffering from cancer, protests the addition of known carcinogens to an area widely used as a public playground. Someone else mentions the damage that mercury and lead can wreak on the human body. I speak for the canvasbacks and the other deep divers feeding on small creatures that find their own sustenance in river-bottom sediments and thus may begin the transmission of poisons up the food chain. Speaker after speaker stresses the desirability of exploring alternatives to direct water discharge: Where there are people, there shall be wastes, but let's think about how we'd handle the stuff if there were no river, no creek, no water at all to dump it in. What about recycling or composting treated wastes? What about land applications? Such technology not only exists but is utterly practicable and widely used. The DEM's hearing panel listens but does not ask questions nor even nod in acknowledgment of any point. Indeed, its members look bludgeoned by the loud but calm and unanimous force of the public's *NO*. We the people are well aware, of course, that the hearing is a minor skirmish in the big war. Yet, when the hearing ends, we are—not jubilant, exactly, but grinning and daring to hope that common sense might just prevail.

New Year's again. In winter 1991, the river runs free from ice. Marsh ducks remain in the pond's secluded bays; the water in our front yard is host to troupes of buffleheads and ruddy ducks. And the most colossal flights of red-breasted mergansers that we've ever seen whizz downriver just over the surface. The canvasbacks are also present, but only in their normal complements, six here, ten there, and they ride the water so far out that I can identify them only by turning my spotting scope to its full magnification. The cans' appearance by the thousands had been a fluke of the weather, the record-breaking freeze that had barred them from more northerly wintering sites.

And at New Year's 1991, the question of Cherry Point's permit, yea or nay, is still in the air. We wait.

An indication of the direction the answer may take comes in May—this time by word of mouth rather than by classified ad too small to notice, much less to read. An ad will appear eventually in public print, but it's our neighbor Mo who tells us that he's heard bad news. It was confirmed soon afterward by others, including a wildlife biologist with the U.S. Forest Service, who has seen and read the environmental assessment (EA) asserting that Cherry Point's application does not require an environmental impact study

(EIS). An EA, which gives an overview of ecological considerations, is made to determine whether a particular project warrants a full-scale EIS before the decision is made to let the project go onstream or to consign it to oblivion. In this case, a discharge of three and a half million gallons is scheduled to go not only onstream but right smack-dab in it. And what of the water-skiers, swimmers, and boaters? What of the fish and the crabs and the tiny, bottom-of-the-food-chain organisms that live in the mucky sediments? What of the bald eagle, an endangered species, that flies this coast with fortunately increasing frequency—and preys on fish? What of the deep-diving ducks? What, especially, of the canvasbacks?

I ask questions. A senior scientist with the North Carolina Environmental Defense Fund shakes his head and offers an opinion earned by long experience. He says that when it comes to issuing permits for such things as waste discharges, the Environmental Protection Agency and the U.S. Fish and Wildlife Service are at loggerheads about the need to consider species officially designated as threatened and endangered. The EPA, he believes, has placed critters at the bottom of its priority heap, and the agency's political clout, along with its size, gives it a great edge over Fish and Wildlife. Nor does such polarized disagreement occur only at the federal level; the efforts of always underfunded, always understaffed state agencies are pulled apart by the same contradictory tensions. Money, of course, plays a big part in deciding how best to handle a problem. Where shall we put the wastes we create? Often, the resolution arrived at is the short-term resolution that calls for the lowest initial outlay of dollars. And the critters get lost in the shuffle—not only the species that are hanging onto earthly existence by the slimmest threads, not only those that are considered of special concern or significantly rare (designations that call for protection and vigilance), but those that are such downright common creatures that no one sees fit to afford them special care or even much attention. That category includes starlings, Norway rats, copperheads, mosquitoes and ticks, and us.

Winter 1992. In January, most of the ducks raft so far out on the river that I cannot see if canvasbacks are among them. Only the tiny buffleheads and an occasional red-breasted merganser work close to shore. In February, on the third, the state formally grants Cherry Point a permit to build the new wastewater outfall that will discharge directly into the river. Contracts for its construction will be awarded in March 1993; a year later, up to three and a half million gallons of new and diverted effluents will start flooding straight into the Neuse every day (and Sunday is no day of rest). But to mourn for the river this soon may be premature. Is it foolish to hope that there's still time to find healthy solutions to waste-disposal problems and to come up with visionary remedies for the chronic shortsightedness of humankind?

Nor am I quite ready to mourn for the canvasbacks. It's hard, though, to be sanguine about their lease on the future. The species' all-or-nothing adherence to tradition may be as devastating as drought and predators, guns and toxic chemicals. And it's even harder to admit, to face the natural fact, that despite broad knowledge, sophisticated skills, and the most altruistic intentions, my species may not be able to help the canvasbacks. We can clean up the waters, fly to the moon, transplant a heart, but we cannot reprogram a bird. More often than not, the greater world outside ourselves insists on having its own way.

Once, though, for two weeks in a frigid January, that world gave us canvasbacks by the thousands and tens of thousands: an unspoiled, wayward gift.

For information on the Adopt a Pothole Program, contact:
North American Wildlife Foundation
102 Wilmot Road, Suite 410
Deerfield, Illinois 60015
(708) 940-3739

Crows of the Sea

On March afternoons, the pale sky to the south bursts open without a sound and flings uncountable streamers over North Carolina's river Neuse. Narrow, sooty-dark, and incredibly long, they flutter, ripple, coil and uncoil, rise and descend, sometimes almost touching the iron-grey water, as some invisible force hurls them northward toward the river's mouth. Every afternoon, all afternoon, they come, streamer on living streamer: double-crested cormorants by tens, perhaps hundreds, of thousands.

Where do they come from, these cormorants flying in mile-long single files? What are they doing? And why? Two weeks before the spring equinox and two weeks afterward, they appear soon after the noon meridian and wing their determined way downriver almost till dusk. Never do we see them flying upriver, not early in the day nor late. Nor do they fly in the fashion described in the field guides. The books have it that the double-crested species often moves from hither to yon in V-shaped wedges like those of ducks and geese, and that it's generally given to cruising at an altitude somewhat higher than that preferred by other kinds of cormorants. But these birds fly low for the most part, often skimming the waves in ribbonlike bill-to-tail columns only one bird wide. I put my questions to some of the area's more knowledgeable bird-watchers. They have no explanations. They don't even seem to be curious about this daily explosion of birds, which is silent, enormous, and certainly odd. One man, however, does say in an offhand way that cormorants are migratory, but this behavior doesn't strike him as part of a migration pattern.

His remark prompts me to guess that at this time of year the cormorants' migration to summer breeding grounds is largely done. They are on location, but the labor of nesting has not yet co-opted every minute of their time, every spark of their energy. And interim, these birds, which are gregarious by nature, become commuters that travel by one route to the day's work of fishing and return by another to their nighttime roosts. But I find no confirmation for this guess. Where, what, and why—the search for answers produces frustration, not facts. What's needed now is balm for the raging itch of unsatisfied curiosity, and I know where to look for that—in the unscientific realms of literature and the lexicon. I can also consult the evidence that flies, swims, and perches most abundantly before my eyes.

One of the first things learned is that I disagree with the poet Shelley. Telling what cormorants are, he more truly tells what cormorants are not. He writes in "The Witch of Atlas" of the bird at a storm-battered lake where the high winds and hail have

> Ploughed up the waters, and the flagging wing
> Of the roused cormorant in the lightning flash

> Looked like the wreck of some wind-wandering
> Fragment of inky thunder-smoke—. . . .

The simile is lovely but insubstantial as a ghost. Yes, the ribbons and streamers of cormorant flight seem to wander and flutter on the river's winds. Yes, the feathers of adult birds shine wetly black as fresh ink. But smoke, even the cold, dank, sullen smoke of a tattered thundercloud—no, no, no! The cormorant is not—and has never been—so lacking in substance and volition.

The second thing I learn is that all the cormorants in the world, all thirty-three species found in both the New World and the Old, were long ago mislabeled. Their English common name seems appropriate for a large, black bird: The word *cormorant* condenses the Latin phrase *corvus marinus*, crow of the sea. And, like crows flocking on a field to glean grain, they flock by the dark dozens on the water to fish. Sometimes they raft almost as thickly as ducks, though anyone watching them swim would never mistake them for waterfowl. Ducks ride the water like buoyant little boats, but cormorants are submarines, their feathered hulls immersed, their backs awash, their heads atop the long slender necks upthrust like periscopes. Nor does their posture in flight resemble that of ducks or crows; though a cormorant's flight path runs basically parallel to the earth or water below, the bird itself flies at a cattywampus angle, its head held ten to fifteen degrees higher than its stubby tail. But, crow of the sea— though that name lacks literal accuracy, it's not really a wrong name, for it has the imagination-satisfying impact of a good metaphor.

The birds' misnomer lies hidden, harmlessly so, in *Phalacrocorax*, the name chosen for the single genus that encompasses every one of the thirty-three species. The *corax* part is fitting and just; it's the name that the classical Greeks, Aristotle among them, used for both cormorants and ravens. (The crow-cormorant association must surely be as ancient as humankind's first awareness of these large, jet-black birds.) The trouble comes with *phalacros*, a Greek word meaning "bald-headed." As we know, as the Greeks most certainly knew, cormorants do not have raw and naked pates. The Greeks, however, did recognize another bird to which they gave the name *phalacrocorax*, "bald-headed crow"—the bald or hermit ibis, which has a large, dark, corvine body but a head as red and featherless as that of a vulture. But in medieval Europe, for reasons that very likely have to do with *corax* as a word denoting both crow and cormorant, the name of the ibis slid onto the cormorant, and there, hallowed by the taxonomists if not by the classicists, it remains to this day.

The double-crested birds we see on the river today, that twice I have touched, congregate, the more the merrier, and play at statues, perching bolt upright on pier pilings. Though the webbed feet are broad and the legs seem almost disproportionately short, the bodies are streamlined and the necks slender and heron-like. At rest on the pilings, the birds tilt their heads upward and hold their long, hook-tipped bills in the air at a slightly supercilious angle. At the base of each bill the naked skin of the throat pouch gleams orange-gold in brilliant contrast to the dark feathers. Sleek-headed immature birds have charcoal-brown backs and creamy bellies dotted amply with cinnamon freckles. The adults wear plumage that is the color of midnight water frosted with the faintest lace of moonlight or foam. Only breeding adults sport the double crests, which many field guides do not adequately illustrate. Drawings and photographs often give the impression that "double" means two slight prominences on a single crest that really looks more like a wind-tousled cowlick. Though "crest" seems far too grand a word for a small sprouting of delicate, threadlike feathers, our cormorants indeed have two such tufts, one on each side of the head, like the "ears" of some owls and the "horns" of a grebe. And as the birds perch, both the young and their breeding elders may unfold wings and give them full spread in the open posture that heraldry calls "displayed." The purpose is to air-dry feathers that have become waterlogged from immersion while fishing.

Cormorants—not just those with double crests but all species—are piscatorial experts. It was in this role that the idea of cormorant, though not the bird itself, was introduced to my four-year-old attention. At that time and for decades afterward, till I saw my first live specimen flying over the river, I associated cormorants with China and, more particularly, with a small fishing boat on the yellow waters of the Yangtze River. The source of this exotic but parochial misapprehension was a children's book, still in print after sixty years,

called *The Story About Ping,* written by Marjorie Flack and illustrated by Kurt Wiese. Ping, a duckling, lived with his parents, siblings, aunts and uncles, and forty-two cousins aboard a wise-eyed
boat—a vessel with eyes painted on either side of the bow, like an
ancient Greek ship, so that it could see its way ahead. The tale
follows a classic plot: disobedience, punishment, and redemption.
To avoid a light spank for being last to reboard the wise-eyed boat
after a day of hunting with his large family for food in the Yangtze
River, Ping hides and runs away. He gets lost, of course, and has
scary adventures but finally finds his way home and accepts the
spank. What remains most clearly in my memory are the strange
dark birds that Ping encounters as he searches for his own boat and
family. They are cormorants, each with a metal ring placed firmly
around its neck so that it cannot swallow the large fish it catches.
And as the birds deliver their catch to the master of the small fishing
boat, he rewards them with tidbits cut small enough to slide down
their artificially constricted gullets. And to this day, fishing with
cormorants is practiced traditionally in some Far Eastern places.

The river's double-crested cormorants fish only for themselves, of
course. Diving deep, they fly underwater to seek and take their
food—minnows, amphibians, shrimp. It would never occur to anyone at Great Neck Point to collar their efficient energies for human
use. It is, however, because people also occupy themselves at fishing
that I have two times been able to touch these birds. And both times
they were dead: Swimming beneath the river's surface, they had
become entangled in our gill net, and they drowned. From one I
plucked a primary feather. Black as widow's weeds, glistening with
salty river water, it was surprisingly long, nearly spanning the distance between my elbow and my fingertips. Each bird was mourned
with a brief shiver of regret.

But their species calls forth celebration, exasperation, fury, wonder, anything but mourning. Talk of tough old birds—so far as real
birds are concerned, the double-crested sea crows provide a living,
flourishing definition. *Tough* speaks of their adaptability. Fresh water or salt, they are not finicky. Not only do they make themselves at
home on both coasts of the United States, from Maine to the Gulf of
Mexico, from the Aleutians to Baja California, but they frequent the

Great Lakes and the lower Mississippi Valley. *Tough* speaks also of the birds' ability to withstand threats and actual insults to habitat and food supply—the agricultural runoffs, the municipal and industrial wastes discharged in the waters. Not only to withstand but to thrive in the face of these pressures against success. They have thrived, in fact, to such a vigorous extent that some people engaged in commercial fishing have come to regard them as competitors and outright pests. And throughout the South, catfish farmers rage, using their choicest imprecations against the black birds that settle by the hundreds on man-made ponds and gorge themselves right merrily on fish flesh.

And *old*—merely to think of the antiquity of cormorants brings a shudder, the same shudder with which I respond to such scary questions as *What lies beyond the universe?* and *How long is forever?* The answers are far too huge ever to be contained within my understanding. Nor does putting a number on a large concept make it more manageable. Seventy million—how many years is that? The humanly allotted three score and ten multiplied by a cool and utterly incomprehensible million. But, then to now, Ur-cormorant to thirty-three species of *Phalacrocorax,* that is the evolutionary ornithologists' conservative estimate of how long the bird has been in existence as an entity distinct from all others. Its slow, gentle apparition on earth is coeval with the appearances of flowering plants and sequoias, marsupials and the first little mammals. And its anatomy indicates that it, along with the loon and the grebe, is among the most aboriginal of true birds.

March after March, some avian instinct flings long, narrow lines of cormorants into the air like streamers thrown forth in celebration. Where are the birds going? What are they doing? And why? I still don't know, though the list of Carolina birds published by John Lawson in 1709 suggests part of an answer: ". . . we have great Flocks of them with us, especially against the Herrings run, which is in *March* and *April*; then they sit upon Logs of dry Wood in the Water, and catch the Fish." These observations point to a seasonally activated behavior for gathering food. Three hundred springtimes later, the herrings still make spawning runs upriver but not in their former silvery, churning abundance. These days, it's possible that the Neuse's cormorants outnumber its herrings.

Where, what, why? It's only my head that wants to understand. My heart knows these questions are puny. In a time out of mind, in a time before the conception of time, there were cormorants flying in fluttering, rippling, coiling and uncoiling, lovely ribbons toward now and tomorrow.

A Bird in the Hand

The belted kingfisher in my hands: a warm cloud of feathers, sooty blue-grey above, white below, a bright hint of rust edging bellyward just under the point at which wings join the body. Blue-grey bands the breast, white collars the short thick neck, blue spurts from the massive head in a ragged crest. The bill is an ivory lance as long and stout as my little finger. The black eyes glitter, wary. But the bird does not struggle nor feint with its bill. It does not even quiver. My palms cup the rapid beating of its heart.

Its size astonishes. It looks not much bigger than swallow or sandpiper as it flies over the wide and salty river that flows past my front door. Hunched on a snag or a piling, it seems no bigger than a robin. Distance deceives, and so does the bird's shape, great shaggy head dwarfing the stub-tailed body. Though the kingfisher feels as weightless as a puff of smoke, its size is nearly that of a crow.

All morning and all afternoon, this kingfisher and one other chattered along our September shore, zipping upriver, down, back up again. Though they must have taken time-out to hover and dive for food, their noisy to-and-fro flights have seemed continuous, suggesting play—a grand game of chase that had started at sunup and would cease only when sundown said okay kids, time for bed. But the game ended with forty-five minutes of good daylight left. The halt came abruptly, rudely. On a fast swing upriver, both birds swooped low over the river's surface, and one fell in. Nothing unusual about kingfishers plunging into the water—they collect their fishy dinners by diving in bill first and rising again. This one, however, did not. The Chief and I watched it from the trailer's doorway and, watching still, moved out on the deck, went into the yard. The bird in the water was swimming. The bird in the air hovered, called, flew down to check its teammate, flew up, and repeated these motions half a dozen times before it proceeded elsewhere. At first, it appeared that the swimmer was headed toward the riverbank for a firm footing, and a takeoff well before sunset. We cheered it shoreward. But the bird moved awkwardly. It spun in loose, tipsy little circles and made little headway. Then, current or clumsiness or fatigue caused it to turn around. Inch by slow inch, it left land behind. And the sun was slipping down, staining the water crimson. Small bird on vast river—we could not bear to watch another minute. I pulled on a jumpsuit, grabbed a dip net, and waded out.

And the bird is ashore now, warm and unresisting in my hand. It's larger than life, and not just in close-up proportions. In the beat of the kingfisher's heart, I also feel the pulse of myth. I hold the halcyon.

Aristotle wrote of the halcyon's power. Though an uncanny accuracy usually marks his observations of the natural world, his tales of the halcyon bear the stamp of myth. Most birds, he says, breed in spring or summer, but not the halcyon. It chooses instead the harshest time of year, the winter solstice. But the gods give aid; they put to sleep the prevailing northerlies and send in gentle breezes from the south for fourteen days—the seven needed for the bird to build her nest, the other seven for the laying and hatching of her five eggs. A gift of calm amid hibernal storms, the rolling and breaking seas made still, made safe for sailors and traveling merchants—this is a holy interlude, the halcyon days.

Such dulcet rumor has enjoyed a long and hallowed life. Long before Aristotle's time, a story related the origin of the halcyon days. Alcyone was daughter to quick-moving, changeable Aeolus, king of the winds. She married Ceyx, son of the Morning Star. And they lived happily, but not ever after, for Alcyone compared their earthly wedded bliss to that in heaven and, in the wild abandon of pillow talk, dared call herself Hera and her husband Zeus. Predictably, the Olympian couple felt themselves denigrated by the comparison, and they sought to put the upstarts in their place. That winter, leaving Alcyone at home, Ceyx sailed off to consult an oracle. Seizing their chance when it came along, the king and queen of the gods arranged for a storm at sea. A monstrous wave broke over Ceyx's ship and washed him overboard. When Alcyone received the news of his drowning, her grief rose so huge and unappeasable that she attempted to join him by throwing her own body into the sea. But a god of the unassuming sort that does anonymous good works showed his pity by turning Wind's daughter and the son of the Morning Star into kingfishers. And from that time to this, the female kingfisher, chattering her sorrow, carries her dead mate's body out to sea. The wintry waves grow calm to receive him. When the waters close over his feathers, she builds a nest, launches it, and lays her eggs as soon as land is out of sight.

Thanks to Pliny, the Roman natural historian, we have a description of Alcyone's mythical nest. It is a round, hollow ball that may be entered through a narrow, projecting mouth. It looks like a sponge, and some people think it's made of sea foam. The substance is so dry and tough that it cannot be cut by a knife, though a hard blow may break it apart.

Halcyon days. Now who would be so rudely skeptical as to think it mere coincidence when calm spells visit the Mediterranean Sea at the time of the winter solstice? They're part of the normal weather. Did they not, however, originate through Alcyone's grievous needs? But her tragedy is largely forgotten. Now she is only a name without body or history. Halcyon: Like its namesake, the word has undergone metamorphosis, serving as an adjective that shines with visions of the idyllic or providing the noun that designates the species of a quite real bird.

But the kingfisher she became is with us not only as the chattering bird that hovers and dives for fish. It is present also as the spirit bird that wings and preens in centuries of poems. Three hundred years after Aristotle, the Latin poet Virgil placed kingfishers on an intimate basis with divine energies; they were *dilectae Thetidi alcyones,* "pets of the sea-nymphs." And the rumor that kingfishers charmed the seas crept with marveling appreciation into English poetry. Typical are Joshua Sylvester's early seventeenth-century lines:

> And the king's-fisher, which so builds her nest
> By the seaside in midst of winter season
> That man, in whom shines the bright lamp of reason,
> Cannot devise with all the wit he has,
> Her little building how to raise or raze:
> So long as there her quiet couch she keeps,
> Sicilian sea exceeding calmly sleeps,
> For Aeolus, fearing to drown her brood,
> Keeps home the while, and troubles not the flood.

Sylvester, of course, observes the emblematic bird, the bird that promises calm to human beings as well as to water, and he sees the Wind-Father as granting a period of grace to the presumptuous daughter who dared compare herself to deity. Several decades later, Andrew Marvell, he of the coy mistress, uses the fabulous name to look at the real bird:

> The modest halcyon comes in sight
> Flying betwixt the day and night.

Worldwide, close to ninety species of kingfishers fly betwixt day and night. Of all this rackety, fleet-winged tribe, only the belted kingfisher—the bird that Audubon would have named the United

States kingfisher—is found in eastern North America, and it alone bears Alcyone's name. In the traditional Latinate binomial *Megaceryle alcyon, mega* means great, and *ceryle* is a general term used by long-gone Greeks to refer to a probably mythical seabird. (Recently, in the cause of some mysterious nomenclatorial housecleaning, *mega* has been dropped.) *Alcyon* of course makes whispered remembrance of a desolate, determined queen.

Fall, winter, and spring, the river's halcyons follow the shoreline in clattering flight or perch on a branch, a piling, an electric power line above the water. They prefer to station themselves in open places that cast no shadows to obscure the water's surface and the tasty morsels swimming below. When they fly looking for fish, they may scan the water from heights as great as thirty feet. And, prey found, they tuck in their wings, aim their large bills straight down, and strike like homing missiles. Fish make up the main part of their diet, but they'll also sustain themselves on other foods—aquatic delicacies such as oysters and mussels, terrestrial tidbits like salamanders, mice, and baby birds. Reliable observers also report that they sometimes behave like flycatchers, taking moths and butterflies on the wing.

But in June and July, as summer bubbles and comes to a steamy boil, the halcyons of Great Neck Point virtually disappear. On rare occasions, one or two birds may grant a random display, but the rest are gone. Though belted kingfishers are as monogamously faithful as Alcyone during their breeding season, they have not heeded Aristotle. Each mated pair has flown elsewhere to excavate a burrow nest in a bank above water, a job that may take from a few days to two weeks. And they incubate their five to eight eggs for slightly more than three weeks. Nor are the nests tidy but reek of decomposing fish. Only when the young are fledged do kingfishers reappear in numbers along our waterfront.

Their flight traces exactly the contours of our shore. It seems as if their rapid rattle calls sew a tightly stitched seam betwixt the water and the land. And in winter, when the birds are most visible and loud, the northerlies do sometimes sleep. The whitecaps vanish, the river purls and sparkles, and people leave their storm-sealed dens to go outside, to open themselves to sun and the noisy presence of kingfishers. It is quite reasonable then to associate our *alcyon* with smiling calm. It is quite possible to believe again in summer.

The sun is down. In gathering darkness, I put warm, almost weightless myth on the trailer's deck. Fly away, fly! I think the bird is young, one of this summer's brood. The dazzling, day-long exhibition—upriver, down again—*was* play and, at the same time, a serious exercise in acquiring grown-up skills. I also think the bird might be female. Reversing the usual avian style of couture, drab hen and gaudy cock, the female belted kingfisher wears richer plumage than the male. Below her smoky blue-grey breast band, she sports a stomacher the color of rust or red clay. This bird that I've held shows traces of such ripe feathering, the beginnings perhaps of fully adult garb.

Fly, bird, fly! But it does not take wing. It crouches on stumpy legs and turns its great head to look first at me, then at the Chief. Though no splinter of bone pokes through the feathers and no blood shows, it may be hurt. Was a wing bruised on sudden contact with the water? What shall we do with you, bird?

Luckily, there is a resource, the Outer Banks Wildlife Shelter, located not, hallelujah, on the Outer Banks, those impossibly distant barrier islands, but only a hop and a jump away in Morehead City. And volunteers man the shelter till 9:00 P.M. While the Chief keeps an eye on the feathered drop-in, I use the telephone. We are instructed to put the bird in a cardboard box. The darkness of such an enclosure will serve to induce and maintain quiescence. Come daylight, if the bird is still alive, we are to bring it in for examination and further care.

In the morning, the bird is very much alive. It hops in the box and glares at me balefully. Its ivory mandibles close on my index finger as if it were a fish. I see that there's been a definite injury: A streak of dried blood mats the feathers below the right wing. I close the box, and off we go.

The volunteer at the shelter's front desk opens the box and takes a peek. "So big!" she says. "I've never been this close to one before." Then she bids me call the next day to see how the kingfisher fares.

It does not survive. Not only was a bone in the right wing broken, but the droppings contained much blood, a sign of severe internal injury. It must have occurred on the bird's sudden, unplanned impact with the river. Water appears to be soft, but hit the wrong way, it's hard as a boulder.

A bird in the hand—I'm grateful for the opportunity, though ill chance brought it about. But it's brutally clear that the hoary adage has got the truth backwards. A bird in the hand is never worth two in the bush, in the nest, in the free-ranging air.

The Woman and the Poppycock

Sooner or later Aesop had to show up at Great Neck Point. It may have been fated, this appearance of a fable-spinning moralist among the ancient poets and natural historians I usually consult in matters pertaining to critters. Aesop? I certainly haven't expected him, much less imagined that he'd come disguised as my neighbor Lana. It all begins as Sal and I walk from the pond road into her yard.

"I have a bird story for you," she calls. Dressed for a trip to town, she already has her hand on the car door. She climbs in, starts the engine, and rolls down the window to holler, "And it's the truth!"

Curiosity flaps its wings. Any bird story told by Lana has got to be a doozy. It's got to involve a bird so large, so loud, so colorful, so totally out of the ordinary that it overcame her customary indifference to birds in general and insisted on being noticed. Not only noticed but remembered.

At best, Lana pays only cursory attention to the feathered tribes. Her environs bear three acknowledgments of their existence. One is the small feeding station nailed to a sweet gum near the front porch of the house in which she lives with her husband Joe and their newly teenaged daughter. Cowbirds use the feeder as a winter hangout. Then, the remnants of a bluebird box, built and erected by a neighbor, dangle from a pole at the edge of the neatly mowed lawn and a bushhogged field that Joe sometimes uses for growing melons. During the first year of its installation, the box housed two successive broods of bluebirds, but at the beginning of the second, it took the full force of Lana's .410 shotgun, with which she'd blasted away the rat snake sliding into the entrance hole with its appetite set on bluebird eggs. The third acknowledgment floats on the drainage pond dug in her back field. There she has installed a mixed raft of ducks—the pintail and scaup decoys that Joe used to set out in his waterfowl-hunting days. Drifting lazily at the ends of their weighted tethers, the decoys do not at all perturb the drainage pond's resident slider turtles and bullfrogs, the visiting green-backed herons, and the constant mourning doves. As Lana says, this postage-stamp pond is the Point's biggest birdbath. At dawn and dusk, the doves and grackles, indigo buntings, grosbeaks, and bluebirds flock here to wet their whistles and give their feathers the water treatment. Barn and rough-winged swallows skim over the algae-green surface to hunt insects or scoop up drinking water on the wing. And sometimes birds less commonly seen stop for a moment on the red-clay banks—a solitary sandpiper or a greater yellowlegs during spring migration, an immature, white-feathered little blue heron during the fall. I doubt that Lana is able to call many of these birds by name.

What can she possibly have to tell? What bird, what event is so extraordinary that she's already found it necessary to insist on her story's truth? It apparently contains some element that others have found a bit hard to believe.

But then, when it comes to birds, anything might happen at Great Neck Point. We're located on a latitude at which northern and southern species intermingle. We're on the Atlantic flyway; migrants land and sometimes linger here for a month in spring or fall before they resume their journeys. And more than a fortunate fluke in geography brings birds our way: Passing cold fronts often activate broad-bladed northerly winds that shovel everything—birds, fish, piers—willy-nilly upriver. We see birds that aren't supposed to be here. In winter, storms may push in such oceanic rangers as the black-legged kittiwake. A half-gale deposits Nashville warblers in the shrubbery during spring as well as fall migrations. Once a hard blow brought in a bird common farther south but regarded in these parts as a rare accidental—the reddish egret. It perched on a half-rotten piling near shore for thirty minutes, quite long enough for my amateur eye to discern that it was not the somewhat similar adult little blue heron, which is not infrequent on this shore. At Great Neck Point, the unexpected comes along with almost metronomic regularity. It doesn't matter what the field guides say is possible. The lesson has been learning to trust what I can see.

And what I cannot see. The river is so wide, the woods so dense and shadowy, the sky so vast that their natural and incalculable reaches might shelter anything from prying sight. They hide nothing, however, from imagination's eyes. Each day, the sun rises like a phoenix from the ashes of night. And why might there not be a phoenix here? At least one representative of a legendary genus certainly flies along this river shore—the halcyon, a bird well known to Aristotle. Nowadays, we have forgotten its queenly, sorrowful past and call it the belted kingfisher. But by any name, this bird is myth incarnate.

And, if myth is made tangible in one of the Point's birds, it is also reasonable for me to make the leap toward faith in what I cannot see. Take the phoenix. For its history and habits, Pliny the Roman serves as Audubon, as Roger Tory Peterson. Native to Arabia, one—and only one—phoenix exists in the world at any one time. Though it's large as an eagle, it hides itself so well that human eyes have rarely glimpsed its splendor. But those who have been fortunate enough to see the great bird say that gold shines below its tufted throat to ornament the royal purple of its body. The tail spreads blue, embellished with rose-colored feathers, and a crest crowns the head. Sacred to the Sun, its representative and acolyte, the bird lives 540 years. When life begins to ebb, it builds a nest made fragrant with cinnamon and frankincense and lies there till it dies. Then, out of its bones and marrow, a grub appears and, as it grows, becomes a chicken, which carries the parental nest to a pyre on the altar of the Sun. As soon as this filial duty has thus been accomplished, there is an explosive and dazzling transformation: Modest fowl becomes the reigning phoenix.

Pliny's view of the phoenix was confined, of course, to his own time, nor was he aware of the New World. But, just as the halcyon finds a suitable habitat at Great Neck Point, so might the phoenix. All year, dawn and sunset hint at the bird; their plumed clouds are emblazoned with its colors. The Point can also meet some of the bird's other conditions: The river in summer offers incendiary sun, and the land provides sweet alternatives for cinnamon and frankincense—honeysuckle and the bay-scented leaves of wax myrtle. And if the phoenix is possible here, then angels indeed may hover overhead, along with a host of equally aerial, hard-to-spot creatures with wings.

The Greeks have provided a lively catalogue of volatile beings. Of its many entries, I can definitely spot the wingèd horse Pegasus among the stars. With luck, I may catch sight of his earthly inversion the Pegasus bird, the only equine feature of which is its horse's head. Then, the river might offer refuge to the *kepphos* mentioned by Aristotle, a seabird that snaps at the foaming waves and somewhat resembles a gull or a tern. It's easy to catch if it's sloshed with salt water, and the bird is well worth catching because, though the rump and tail reek of shoreweed, the flesh is plump and succulent. Another bird well known to the ancients must surely be housed at the Point—the phallos bird. Its body is that of a domestic goose; its head and neck, an erect penis with a wattle of testicles at the point where the neck of a real goose joins its breast. Athenian vases picture this bird as a cosseted ladies' pet. (And so it should be, said the seer Teiresias, who spent at least seven years of his life as a woman and knew from lusty experience what he was talking about—that women take nine times more pleasure in sex than do men.) The skies at the Point may hold birds less easily domesticated: scavenging harpies; wingèd griffins with hooked, eagle-like beaks and the bodies of lions; and Sirens, those soft, sweet-singing, fatal birds with women's heads.

By the time I catch Lana, I'm ready for anything. I knock on her door one evening after she's come home from work. She invites me into the kitchen, where a talk-show hostess smiles and babbles from a six-inch TV and the table, not yet laid for supper, is strewn with cross-stitch patterns and a rainbow of embroidery floss. "Sit down," she says. "Let me tell you about the rooster."

Rooster! What is this? I'm psyched for a rare accidental, if not an outright miracle. But it looks as if what I'm going to get will be something out of Aesop, who specialized in fables featuring foxes and mice and other unexciting, all too common, plain-Jane creatures.

Lana smiles disarmingly. "Now listen. And let me tell you right now it's the truth."

It would be impolite to get up and leave. Obediently, I sit.

She begins her tale in the storyteller's time-old fashion by dating it with an event rather than the month and the year. "I was pregnant with my daughter, my last child. I was ill, but I'd worked hard to plant a garden, and the beans were just starting to come in on the vines. I dreaded canning them because we did not have an air-conditioner, but I did enjoy doing a few at a time for supper.

"Now, that summer someone gave my husband's brother some fighting cocks—Araucanas, mean, long-spurred Cubans. They lay blue eggs, the hens do, but these were roosters and they were really mean. Joe's brother was putting them in my chicken pen till he got his built. But the roosters kept getting out of my pen, and he had not made any progress in making one of his own. So I told him, I said, 'If they start getting into my garden, you're going to be minus some fowls.'

"And sure enough, soon as the beans came on the vines, the roosters got out and started pecking. They don't eat beans. They just ruin them. They go along and peck a little bit, go on to the next one and peck a little more.

"One day I had chased one rooster I don't know how many times out of the bean patch. It was late afternoon, and here he was again, just coming right back down through the vines. And every time he'd take a snip of bean, he'd crow like he was doing the greatest thing. I loaded up my shotgun and went out there—you've had it, buster. He was between the rows, and he stuck his head up to crow. He got out exactly half a crow before I gave him a good shot with a number-three shell. And he fell out. Of course, I blew up half the bean patch. I destroyed more beans than any rooster could've. A whole herd of roosters couldn't have done that much damage. But he fell out half through his crow, and he was dead.

"I'd already had a cow butchered that morning. When Joe came home that afternoon, his daddy hollered at him. He said, 'Joe, that woman's gone crazy. She called the slaughterhouse to kill a cow today. Now she's shot a rooster. If you don't act right, you may be next.'

"When Joe came in, I told him what I'd done and why. And I told him, 'You better go out there and bury that rooster.' He dug a hole under the pear tree, picked the rooster up, and threw him in. That rooster had been lying there good and dead for over an hour. But when he landed in the hole, he finished his crow. And that, I swear it, is the truth!"

Well, I've just heard a cockamamie tale, a real cock-and-bull—no, cock-and-cow—story. I've met the poppycock himself.

Lana reads my doubt and declares most sternly, "That *is* the truth, so help me."

Oh. I do know what happened. When that cocky, marauding bean spoiler landed—thump!—in his grave, the force of collision with firm earth expelled the air or the accumulated gases from his carcass. It's fair to say that he did indeed complete his gun-aborted yodel. At this moment, however, it wouldn't be fair to blast away the story with an explanation. I simply tell Lana that I can hear that rooster crowing even now. She's satisfied.

And I've learned something more than the facts about the poppycock. Aesop has well and truly been at work. And in the customary fashion, the tale is concluded with a moral: One need not leave home nor the present moment to find the fabulous truth.

The problem is, this moral falls short. I look back through twenty-six centuries and shake my head at the man who told of the lion and the mouse, the grasshopper and the ant, and invented the goose that laid the golden egg. Of all people, Aesop should know that truth comes in many guises. And who's to say what's true, what's as-if true, and what's pure poppycock till evidence of some kind shows up in the bean patch of perception and starts to crow?

Patience! I may see the phoenix after all.

When the Wind Found Shape

My neighbor Dorothy gives a quick shudder when she hears that black vultures have just been seen flying over her roof. Half an hour ago, before she'd returned home from errands, three of them flying low along the riverbank cast swift shadows on the dwellings below as they followed the shoreline upstream. I want to quicken her with my excitement—*black* vultures, not the usual turkeys! Sally Doberman has caught the excitement; she prances beside me. But

Dorothy lifts her eyes heavenward and says in a dry tone, "Buzzards—I hope they don't mean bad luck."

Her head knows perfectly well that the birds portend no misfortune, but flesh makes its customary, unsought response. The sudden shiver, the goosebumps are probably as old as humankind. And why not? Vultures seem to embody ugliness; the heads, disproportionately small for the lumbering bodies, look disgustingly naked, and the collective appetite exhibits a horrid predilection for spoiling meat. Worse, vultures are a memento mori: Where there are vultures, there is—or shall be—death. It's not so much the birds themselves that stimulate a shuddering uneasiness as their uncanny ability to give material form to the idea of a dark angel. Winged and silent, they appear without warning, feast, and are gone. The single constant in their apparitions is mortality. Or so it might seem.

Vultures have certainly suffered from a bad press. Of course, the unfavorable notices over several millennia mirror and reinforce what may be an atavistic human aversion to a creature that fuels itself on carrion. And to its reports the press has often tacked on a moral, one designed to show frail humanity its impotence in the face of divine forces. Listen to the rebuttal God gives Job when the latter protests his suffering and asks that the case against him be stated. In a courtroom that is not a courtroom but a howling storm, the voice of God reviews his grand design, from earth's creation through its wonders—constellations, seasons, the beasts and the birds, among them the vulture. God puts a rhetorical question to Job:

> Do you instruct the vulture to fly high
> and build its nest aloft?
> It dwells among the rocks and there it lodges;
> its station a crevice in the rock;
> from there it searches for food,
> keenly scanning the distance,
> that its brood may be gorged with blood;
> and where the slain are, there the vulture is.

A well-observed, fairly straightforward report, except for the bit about gorging the nestlings on blood (at first they eat the adults' regurgitated food and later dine on flown-in carrion). And to this day, not only imagination but reality can recreate the scene: The bird keeps soaring watch, spies a battlefield or pest-plagued village, and settles heavily to glut itself on death. But, waiting for its moment, it is a far more patient bird than the one described by the Greek tragic playwright Aeschylus in *Prometheus Bound.* A passage toward the play's end prophesies the punishment that awaits the hero for committing the sacrilege of stealing fire from the gods and giving it to mortals. And to this day, imagination's chains bind Prometheus to a craggy mountainside and to this day can see him assaulted by Zeus's wingèd hound, a vulture dripping red gore, that comes unbidden and insatiable every morning to rend the hero's body till flesh flutters in the wind like ragged cloth and to tear at his liver till it yields a black, blood-clotted meal. A horrifying myth, but one not easily shrugged off, for it presents a worst-case scenario. The vulture is ominously premature, coming to Prometheus while he is still alive and capable of suffering excruciating pain.

A bad press, yes indeed. By now, however, it may be apparent that I'm on the side of the angels—not the metaphoric host but angels in their vulturine incarnations. I find the birds worth observation and an admiration that amounts almost to awe. There's more to the vulture story, much more, than the built-in human distaste usually finds it comfortable to contemplate. I admit, nonetheless, to feeling the shudder and having a once-strong urge not even to think about the bird, much less get near it. Luckily, reason kept impulse from triggering flight the one and only time I had a chance for a close encounter with *Cathartes aura.*

Cathartes aura is the euphonious name chosen by the nomenclators to designate the turkey vulture. But before I go into the tale of my nose-to-bill confrontation with a representative of the species, allow me a pause for a brief look at vultures in general. The turkey vulture is not at all the bird that Job, listening to God, saw in mind's eye nor the bird that descended ravening each day on helpless Prometheus. Vultures come in two distinct sorts, New World and Old World. Those of the Old World—lammergeier, cinereous vulture, griffon vulture, many others—are members of the family Accipitridae—the seizers—to which hawks, kites, osprey, and eagles also belong. The New World vultures are granted a family all to themselves, the Cathartidae or purifiers, and their various species number only six, all found in the Americas. Three of the sextet are

North American: the ubiquitous turkey vulture, the somewhat less widespread black, and the California condor. The condor exists on the farthest edge of endangerment, its habitat drastically—humanly—invaded. Fewer than five dozen captive-bred birds now maintain the frangible border between the species' life and its absolute extinction. Not surprisingly, the condor in extremis evokes not the shudder reflex but pity and active concern: There but for some random grace go we.

The word *condor*, if not the bird itself, may have been granted a little grace. Coming to us straight from the Spanish, which picked up the original form from the Quecha Indians of the Andes, the word has never acquired the pejorative connotations of *buzzard* and *vulture*. I doubt that anyone has ever cussed anyone else by calling him an old condor. The word simply hasn't got the necessary hiss and spit. It was the Romans who gave us the opportunity to deprecate others by slinging epithets associated with rapacity and foul habits. Their term *vultur* referred only to the Old World birds but transferred easily to those of the New because the two kinds of carrion eaters show marked similarities in appearance and behavior, if not in anatomical structure. It is legitimate to envision a New World bird while reading Aeschylus or the Book of Job. The word *buzzard* has a somewhat more complex history. And, applied to the New World vultures, it's a misnomer. For the first syllable, the Romans are to blame. One of their words for hawk was *buteo*, which has entered science intact but undergone metamorphosis in common speech. Buteo, with a capital *B*, now names one genus of hawks, which includes the stout, high-wheeling red-tailed and red-shouldered, broad-winged and rough-legged varieties; it is these Buteos that are properly buzzards. English most likely acquired the *buzz-* of its word from French, which softened the *t* and abbreviated the whole to one short, almost affectionate syllable, *buse*. (French offers a delightful proverb of the silk-purse-from-sow's-ear sort: *On ne saurait faire d'une buse un épervier*—you can't make a falcon out of a buzzard.) So much for the first part, but where does the second syllable come from? English tacked on the suffix *-ard*, which expresses scorn and appears most frequently at the end of sneering words, such as *laggard, drunkard, coward*, and *bastard*. And how did the name buzzard come to be plastered on New World vultures? I

don't know. It may have been through the Kleenex phenomenon—
the casualness with which people are wont to appropriate a specific
term and then apply it wholesale across a broad spectrum of similiar
things, from facial tissues to birds. Speculation also suggests that to
an American ear the very sound of *buzzard* better suits a vulture
than a hawk.

The confrontation? Patience. It's coming up right after one more
quick digression into names. Vulture or buzzard, neither word acknowledges the family's vital role in the scheme of things. But the
nomenclators, scientists who had more than a passing acquaintance
with ancient history and practices, reached into the Greek and Roman past and came up with formal terms that not only incorporate
physical description and the shudder reflex but offer the entire family a bit of reverence. Whoever named the family Cathartidae, the
purifiers, knew that in ancient times purification was a priestly func-
tion, a ritual washing away or purging of guilt and spiritual defile-
ment. Granted, vultures are janitors and undertakers, not priests,
and they operate solely in the material sphere. But like the priests,
they simply clean up messes they did not make. (Unlike their less
dependable human counterparts, they never ask for compensation,
though their success record stands at one hundred percent.) The
birds' quasi-sacerdotal role is given recognition in the turkey vulture's genus name *Cathartes*, which means Purifier; *aura*, the designation for its species, is said to be a South American word (though
there's a sneaking chance, the nomenclators being somewhat high-
handed about spelling and the parts of speech, that it could be the
Latin noun for "air" or "heaven"). Physical description, focused
through a narrow-angle lens of language on the bird's head, takes
over in the condor's name, *Gymnogyps californianus*, Naked-Vulture
native to California. It is the black vulture that evoked its nomen-
clator's visions of death. Both the genus name and that for the
species enfold quite concrete pictures. Though some people read
korax—crow—in the genus name, I read *koura* and see the bird as
a Greek woman in mourning, her hair cropped short to demonstrate
grief, her body bundled in a dark robe: *Coragyps atratus*, Shorn-
Vulture clad in black. The image fits—wrinkled, ash-grey head,
feathers dark as a starless night, with only the fingerlike wingtips
showing white. The black vulture flies with wings held straight and

flat as those of eagles, whereas the turkey vulture wheels through the sky and teeters on uptilted wings as if balanced on a beam of air. The adult turkey vulture's head is as red as a true turkey's wattles; the trailing edge of its underwings is silvery white, as if the feathers were powdered by light frost.

Sometimes, Shorn-Vulture does not wait for death but inflicts it. As did the California condor in its glory days, this smaller bird has been known to take live prey. My sheep-raising father reported it killing and eating his newborn lambs. Much more usually, however, the black vulture settles happily for carrion and uses sharp eyes to find it. The turkey vulture, rare among birds in possessing a keen sense of smell, uses its nose.

Soaring the skies to sniff out the lay of the land, turkey vultures are hardly uncommon in the United States and northern Mexico. They are indeed so common, their feeding habits so well known, that they have given my family a verb, *to vultch*. It refers to the time before the appointed supper hour in which people, children especially, circle the kitchen, perch on chairs, and vultch impatiently, waiting for their dinners to die and be served.

Throughout this country, the real turkey vultures, far more self-possessed than children, perch in trees and on fence posts. Sometimes, as they perch, they extend their great wings, holding them partway open as if to bathe in sunlight and warmth. They soar in every high blue precinct of our sky, and with an instinct-programmed regard for other vultures in the same general area, each observes the boundaries of its own quadrant. When food is found, then limits dissolve and all may eat, or at least as many as can crowd aboard the carcass of a cow or deer. Singly, vultures hunker down on small, road-killed animals. En masse, they sometimes form kettles—groups of dozens or even hundreds—that rise and fall and circle through air like water swirling, churning before it comes to a furious boil. Kettling is most apparent in winter as the great birds, leaving behind the separate doings of the day, congregate and pepper the sky as they fly at dusk to their communal roost. In spring, when the gonads swell and the urge to reproduce subsumes all other interests, crowded roosts are abandoned for the more intimate setting of a rocky ledge, a cave, or a fallen log. The mated pair, however, does not take time for nest building; the hen lays her one to three large eggs on a bare surface. Winter, spring, in any season, turkey vultures tend to keep their distance from people, but if someone should locate adult birds with eggs or young and decide to inspect the find, the parents may seem calm and allow a close approach, then—splat! Vultures have been known to erupt, anointing an intruder with well-placed vomit.

I knew nothing of this defensive tactic before I met the turkey vulture on my mother's front porch, nor did I learn of it till several years after. The episode happened not at Great Neck Point but in a small, polite southern town in the Shenandoah Valley, and it happened this way:

"There's a buzzard on Grandmother's porch!" The voice is that of my elder son, sure that his bird-crazy mother will want to see this anomaly. The November day is overcast, with gusting winds that bear arrows of cold. I think I'd rather stay inside, but curiosity and a slight uneasiness insist that I don heavy jacket and scarf to walk eight houses up the street. It *is* freakish that a countryside scavenger, forsaking its usual haunts, should alight on a porch only one chilly block up the hill from the downtown business district. My mother's house is also a place in which wildness has ever been kept at bay with paint, hot water, medicines, and pep talks on manners. But the bird is indeed there. It stands beside a wooden rocking chair and presses back against the house's grey-painted bricks as I approach. It is as if the November wind has found shape—hulking dark grey, bill ready to rip, the stare as raw as the efficient, naked head. The bird hunches itself, hisses like a threatened cat, but makes no attempt to escape. An omen, surely: Someone is dying.

The 1840s house that is now my mother's has known death—the judge who reared six daughters within its stout walls, my father who died on the sofa bed near the huge fireplace in the library-television room that had been a detached kitchen in the nineteenth century. His bones, now ashes, are buried beneath the Norway maple that he himself planted on the upper back lawn. A bronze plaque marks his grave. Whose death is next?

I take a step. The bird glowers only four feet away. Another step, but the bird shudders and staggers. The charcoal wings that could span six feet flap, hitting the rocking chair and the light-grey bricks. There is no height here, no breadth, no air current to help its heavy body lift. Then it leaps to the iron porch railing and gives the wings their dark spread. They tatter the air and carry that fearful appetite to the garage roof, where, bill agape, it pants like a winded dog. Its eyes seem to gouge holes in everything they see. And I watch as the torn wings beat, trying for steadiness, trying for flight. It stumbles into the air again and descends into the Norway maple, where it rests, somehow made small, no portent but a clump of feathers, flesh, and hollow bones powered by a fierce but willy-nilly failing taste for life. Let it be, give it peace, honor its lesson. Slowly, I walk back home.

The bird is not, has never been, a harbinger of woe. It is only what it is, a feathered carrion eater, no less usefully and ingeniously engineered than other scavengers—hyena, crab, bone-cleaning ant. Its appearance means nothing more than bird at work, hastening to or actually performing its real job in the real world. And if it seems repulsive in its relish for putrefaction and its utter lack of fastidious table manners, blame the beholder. People are the squeamish ones, not vultures. Yet we share with them several causes (though only humankind would denominate as a "cause" an action that's automatic to the bird). One, for a happily growing number of my kind, is an interest in tidiness, in trying to provide good housekeeping for the planet. The other, the common bedrock urge, is to promote the well-being of our individual selves and so, secondarily, the good health of the species.

This morning's black vultures—why the excitement? They skimmed so low over Dorothy's house that Sally gave chase. Lately, she's noticed low-flying vultures; ears perked and eyes aloft, she'll run beneath a flight path till her game is stopped short by a fence or a viney thicket. Sometimes, exhibiting something that looks like puzzlement at the dog's behavior, the bird will circle, seeming to inspect her. Always, till today, the vultures that she's chased have been turkey vultures.

But these were *black!* I've seen them at other times in other places but never before at the river. A new bird, species number 205, for the grand list at Great Neck Point!

Revenant

Doves lead me to a second encounter with the snowy owl—doves cooing softly, improbably in the darkness of a winter night.

A friend led me to the first. An avid bird-watcher, not quite content to stalk and spy out the multifarious species commonly found in August County, Virginia, she keeps her ear to the ornithological hot line and lets me know when something out of the ordinary wings in—a Say's phoebe in the mountains, the red-necked phalarope in a lagoon at the local sewage treatment plant. This time: "Snowy owl, rare accidental, been hanging around now for almost a week. You shouldn't miss it."

She'd already made one pilgrimage and was raring for another. We met the next morning for an iffy excursion. Had the owl flown? Or stayed put? If the answer to the latter question was yes, would we find room to park within a mile of the farm at which it had alighted? The hot line's report of a snowy owl in the Shenandoah Valley had galvanized the twitchers, those do-or-die birders who spring to immediate attention at news of a rarely seen species. Eager to feast on the sight, they'd jumped into their vehicles, sped to the Valley, and converged by the dozens at the hot spot just off county route 608. The mob came not only from every corner of Virginia, but from neighboring states as well—West Virginia, Pennsylvania, the Carolinas. But when we arrived, not one station wagon, van, or scoot-about was parked beside the wire-fenced pasture in which the owl had been observed for the six preceding days. No watchers, no bird to be watched. Or was it simply off hunting? Or had even the most ardent twitchers been kept at their firesides by frigid weather? The temperature was sixteen degrees, reduced by the brisk wind to near zero. Two inches of snow lay on the landscape, and the January sky looked almost as white as the bleak fields below. But we'd made the trip. Refusing defeat, we stopped, climbed out of the car, and started scanning.

The advent in the Valley of a snowy owl is not a once-in-a-lifetime phenomenon. It happens with unpredictable regularity—two years in a row, then the lapse of a decade before another such owl appears. The intervals depend on a cyclic boom or bust—the abundance or scarcity of small rodent prey in the arctic and sub-arctic reaches where the owls live year-round and normally spend the winter. When the larder is well stocked, the owls not only remain in the far north but, fat and happy, increase their numbers. But when an exploded population of owls faces a dwindling food supply, some birds, especially those that are young and thus less skilled at taking a survivor's share of prey, are forced into exile by the bone-bred dictates of their appetites. Such desperate forays to the south are called irruptions—break-ins—as if the owls were sneak-thieves stealing into territory not their own. When they do break into southern regions, they're easy to spot because the species, going against the usual, night-loving grain of owls, does its hunting by day.

We kept scanning: narrow and lonesome country road, a farm set on rolling pastureland, its house, barn, and silos tucked together in close companionship along the sinuous, glittering bends of a small creek. In the near distance, the Blue Ridge Mountains, their trees like rough, black bristles poking through a skin of snow. Close by, an empty, snow-frosted field where cattle were put out to graze in the green heat of summer. We kept scanning that cold, white field for the living whiteness that had summoned us. Go home? Or stay and freeze?

And the sudden bird became material not thirty feet away. It stood on the ground near a clump of high grass and had looked like high grass, dark stems peeking through a coverlet of snow. We had been looking at its back, the bridal feathers brushed with a dark brown, delicate calligraphy. We couldn't see its face. Though it must have been alert to our presence—the slamming car doors, the voices—its gaze was fixed elsewhere. Then its head snapped around in a full half-circle. Frowning, or seeming to frown, the owl turned the yellow beacons of its eyes to stare at us. "O-oh," we whispered, "o-o-oh!" Exhaled breath rolled white on the air, but pleasure pumped heat through shivering flesh. The bird flew then, its wide wings skimming the stiff white grass, and landed on a far fence post. There it perched for a minute or two before it lifted off again and disappeared, hiding its whiteness in a grove of lichened trees. At that we did what the owl could not do: We went home.

A glimpse of something rare and strange, a tantalizing taste—it was enough to whet desire but far from enough to give it satisfaction. Nor did the white barrens of that pasture offer any satiety, not to human eyes, not to the belly of the bird. For two more weeks, the snowy owl lingered amid the glut of observers, then died of starvation. It may have been weakened by its flight for survival; the Valley's abnormally frigid weather may have kept potential prey tucked deep in burrows and warrens. The reason doesn't matter. Nothing could have saved its life. The body was found by a member of the county bird club.

Now, four winters later, the doves make muffled plaint. Every

Tuesday evening for the last three weeks, I've heard their intermittent music. It seeps through a solid wall like slow droplets of water trickling out of a sheer mountain cliff.

The room that I inhabit on Tuesday nights is of the shotgun sort, long enough to hold three tables end to end but barely wide enough for the chairs on either side. Located on the ground floor of the local college's science building, it's a conference room pressed into make-do service as a nighttime classroom. Here, for several winters, I've conducted a completely unscientific workshop for writers. The participants have just been given instructions for a ten-minute exercise in free writing: Write, don't stop, if all you can think of is that you've nothing to say, write that, keep writing it, something will break loose. They scribble furiously. Dove sound oozes through the wall. In my thoughts, the past irrupts.

Once upon an ancient time, doves roosted in the oak trees that shaded Zeus's shrine at Dodona in Greece. Rock doves, turtle doves—no one now knows precisely what species, nor do we need to know. Their importance is that, in the beginning, before Zeus laid claim to the site and its trees, the oak trees were there housing unseen, holy powers. And the doves took on the potent magic of the branches on which they rested: Their soft calls delivered the wisdom of heaven. Priestesses, themselves called "doves," cocked their heads and listened with utmost attention to the cooing in the oak trees. Then they interpreted the fluted oracles and prophecies, putting into plain words all that divinity wished to reveal of its purposes and secret knowledge.

The gods are gone, and the women who understood the talk of birds. But surely the doves remain at Dodona. And from the room that shares a wall with mine, here-and-now doves issue oracles I cannot decode. Nor do the workshop's writers help. Exercise finished, they read aloud the hilarious results. Not one mentions the doves. On we go to talk of tricks for imposing verbal order on the welter of memories, events, and accidents that mark our lives. After the others leave, I tarry to pack up books and papers and tidy the shotgun room. Doves coo.

If there is meaning in their night music, it stays most stubbornly cryptic. Nor can I visit the birds, take a good look at them, for the door to their modern-day shrine is securely locked. I do know, however, that the room is an office, and its tutelary deity is the college's professor emeritus of biology. More particularly, he specializes in ornithology and has for years banded birds, as well as devoting much of his time to such prosaic chores as coordinating the county's annual Christmas Bird Count. I'd almost be willing to give my Audubon print of shoveler ducks for a chance to meet his mysterious doves.

The chance arrives. It comes on the following Tuesday as I idle in the hallway waiting for seven o'clock and the onrush of writers. An overcoated man enters the building, strides to the office door, and unlocks it. He's not the professor. I don't know who he is nor what he's doing here. Who cares? Babbling, "Doves, doves," I barge right in behind him. Ringed turtle doves, three of them! Bodies dressed in feathers of soft beige suggesting pink, dainty half-necklaces of black upon their napes, they shuffle in their cages and coo.

"Pretty things, aren't they," the man says, stepping toward a counter on the wall opposite the doves. He takes something out of his overcoat pockets—looks like two handsful of feathers. Of course, I go to see what he is doing. The feathers turn out to be two eastern screech owls, one a red-phase bird, the other grey. Their rigid bodies are flattened in the shape of tiny coffins; their eyes and bills have been fastened shut by pins with red and yellow beaded heads. He puts these offerings on the counter. And on the counter, a flat black slab that makes me think of an altar, prior offerings expose their breasts, bright pins glistening at eyes and bills like tears or blood: a hooded merganser, a grouse, a red-tailed hawk, an owl.

"Snowy," he says. "Don't hardly see 'em round here. Found dead on a farm out in the country."

Memory swivels full circle and turns its eyes to stare at the white wings brushed with darkest brown, at the belly of untrodden white, the full white buskins on the legs. The talons are curled, gripping overheated office air, piercing the body of this night.

"Four years ago. But how—" Helpless, caught like a mouse, I lift my hands.

"How did it fetch up here?" With a calmness that shows he's unaware the room is haunted, he supplies the facts. The owl's body was taken to the wildlife center located in the county. Having no use for a bird past any sort of rehabilitation, the center handed it on to the professor, who holds a collecting permit. "Illegal, you know, for most folks to keep wild birds, don't matter if they're alive or dead." The professor put the owl, innards and all, in the freezer till he could get around to preparing a study skin. The man has been helping with the preparation. The owl, now gutted and cleaned, has been put out to dry with the other specimens on the counter. No, it won't be stuffed and gussied up with glass eyes to make it look like a living bird. Yes, the pins will remain in its eyes and bill. Where will it end up? He points to the ceiling. "Upstairs, room 213, in a drawer of skins. College girls, they'll get a kick out of something this rare."

Talking, laughing, the writers arrive. I leave to join them. The professor's helper flicks off the light and shuts the shrine's door. From the locked and darkened room, the guardian doves continue ululating mournful prophecies.

Or do they truly make lament? Perhaps they prophesy not only of what is but what shall be: a student examining the skin, stroking the feathers' dry purity, and being lit with a white-hot wonder.

A Place in the Brushpile

The brushpile—that's where Sal and I shall go this morning. Today, no passing clouds cast shadows, no high thin overcast mutes all bright colors to shades of grey. The late September sun, beaming from a sky of seamless blue, promises an ideal light for seeing in finest detail whatever may present itself. And something *will* show in the brushpile, that much is certain. Like fingers exploring a smooth stone, speculation fondles the possibilities. I hope for birds but am willing to settle for anything happenstance brings.

155

And happenstance sometimes presents amazing sights. On a bird-less day last April, I saw small butterflies chasing off a large intruder in the fashion of crows mobbing a hawk. The small ones were the bright and sassy American painted ladies, which fluttered busily over the pile to sip nectar from the myriad white flowers exploding all over the blackberry vines. The stranger was a monarch with dulled colors and ragged wings, a survivor of the long migratory flight from Mexico.

My eagerness is catching. Sal grins and clacks her teeth when she sees me getting ready to go out. She unwittingly delays our depar-ture by spinning herself in tight circles just in front of my shins as I head for the front door. I must either move slowly or trip over a whirling dervish disguised as a dog. Outside, progress is easier. We walk a hundred yards straight inland along a hedgerowed lane, then turn southeast across our neighbor Lana's rough-mowed field that was used three summers ago as a melon patch. Beneath the weeds and tough grasses and crumbling fire ant hills, the soil is ridged like a washboard, long humps where cantaloupes and watermelons were planted, long shallow valleys between the rows. Another hundred yards beyond the far end of these ups and downs the brushpile rises, an oval, ten-by-thirty-foot island in the center of a smaller, flatter field that is surrounded on three sides by woods—not walk-through woods but the kind made humanly impenetrable by an understory densely laced with barbed-wire vines. Sal reaches the brushpile be-fore I do. No birds fly up at her approach. She's sniffing at the pile's perimeter as I slip my sit-upon, as the Chief calls my three-legged stool, from my left shoulder, unfold it, and settle down to wait.

With regularity, I stake out brushpiles. Most of the Point's brush-piles appear at random, jackstraw heaps of bare branches that are tossed together when someone clears a strip of land. Most of them disappear—poof!—in a bonfire burst, leaving nothing behind but their charred ghosts. One such evanescent heap materializes and vanishes several times a year on the floor of a thickety woods that's slowly being thinned. Beneath the remaining trees, a waist-high jumble of trimmings and slender trunks may linger for a month or even a season before it's sacrificed to the flames. While it exists, the birds take every advantage of its nooks, crannies, and abundant perches. At any time of year, calling towhees, the hollering, scolding

Carolina wrens, and cardinals lighting scarlet fires of their own will flock to its latest apparition. In the cold months, it lures wintering sparrows—the commonly seen white-throats, the larger fox sparrows that are much less frequently spotted at the Point.

But this is no come-and-go brushpile that I'm staking out today. It's the Point's biggest, richest, ripest, and bar-none best. The reason for such excellence is that longevity has awarded it substance. This year, not one solitary snaggle of deadwood is visible, though branches and trunks were seminal to the profusion that greets my eyes. When Lana straightened the overgrown edge of her property six years ago, the trashy clutter of felled pines and sweet gums was bulldozed away from woods' edge and heaped up, not for burning but for slow decomposition. Why bother with something that disintegrates all on its own? The dozer blade also scraped soil into the mass so that the wood was lodged atop and partly buried in a knee-high mound of earth. And that was the plinth on which the current brushpile rests. Out of the wood's decay, marvel on small marvel—the minute workings of bacteria, fungi, and boring insects; the building of tiny soil pockets on the recalcitrant clay; the falling to earth of floating or excreted seeds; the rooting of a succession of plant communities, first the annual weeds, then the perennials, and now a few shrubs. Today, the pile rises luxurious, a jungly garden reaching higher than my head. Its next natural stage would be the sprouting and growth of a pine or two—if mortal whim does not suddenly see this brushpile as a pretty awful mess, a hiding place for copperheads and rattlesnakes, and raze the whole thing as if it were a condemned flophouse.

I see it as glorious. Untidy perhaps, but glorious, welcoming, vibrant with colors, sounds, and movements, which reach their peak as September slides into October. The honeysuckle that attracted hummingbirds last May no longer blooms, but the dark green leaves glisten, and bunches of dark berries hang from the vines like minuscule grapes. The blackberry canes bend red toward the rough-cut grass surrounding the heap. Its lower level is studded with sprays of goldenrod flowers, and dog fennel blooms above, its blossom-heavy panicles swaying in the light breeze like gauzy white curtains. Pokeweed thrusting up hither and yon has begun to lose its green leaves, but the magenta stems are laden with dark purple berries.

The shrub that John James Audubon called "Spanish mullbery"—
Callicarpa americana or beauty berry—has claimed the pile's southeast corner; the berries are ripe now and clustered tightly,
abundantly around the woody stems. Landscaping guides suggest
planting Callicarpa to attract and feed birds, and garden catalogues
offer at premium prices this shrub that grows with wild exuberance
on the fringes of the Point's woods. English has no word that catches
exactly the berries' eye-dazzling color, nor can it truly be photo-
graphed. In desperation, the catalogues have settled for "violet purple." Not quite. Throw in a touch of rose and add "electric"—even
so, imagination cannot reproduce the extraordinary hue. It must be
seen. The birds will devour the beauty berries after they've polished
off the poke. In early fall, the brushpile yields hearty pickings to a
good baker's dozen of avian species. And this year, hurray, some
pickings for me! A cherry tomato plant—how did it get here?—
climbs and sprawls vigorously over a natural trellis of honeysuckle,
fennel, and poke. It's loaded with orange-red globes.

But harvesting will come later. The pile is a favorite landing
place, a big rock-candy mountain, a Garden of Eden for fall's feathered migrants. Here and only here have I seen Nashville and
Wilson's warblers. Here I can almost always catch a glimpse of the
otherwise shy house wrens that winter at the Point. Today, I'm sure
that the pile harbors a bird. It makes no sounds but announces its
presence in the snappy spring of topmost leaves as something below
alights or takes off. And flickers of darting movement lead my eye to
the vegetation's shadowy and convoluted depths. It's not a large
bird, not a towhee or a bright-eyed catbird. A sparrow moved in for
the cold months? A migrant heading south? Will it show itself clear?
I've occupied my own perch near the brushpile long enough to have
blended into the landscape and create no startlement. Sally is no
cause for alarm. She long ago finished her exploratory sniffing.
She chased a cottontail—unsuccessfully as usual—and found a
drink in a puddle and came to park beside me on her haunches.
She squeaked softly as if to say, "Let's go." Now she has resigned
herself to my failure to budge; in Doberman fashion, she lies atop
my feet to show me who's really boss. I sit on the three-legged stool
and wait.

And think willy-nilly of ancient Greek oracles, women who acted as intermediaries between the gods and humankind. On duty at the great, temple-bright shrines, they sat on sacred tripods, which were three-legged wooden contraptions designed after the fashion of a molded-metal cauldron with three short legs to elevate it from the ground. Were the tripods as deep as cauldrons? From the ease of my sit-upon's taut seat, I hope not, then ask myself if the oracles would have noticed discomfort. They chewed narcotic bay leaves or, as one rumor has it, inhaled intoxicating vapors that rose from cracks in the earth. In the resultant trance, they listened to the gods and gave inspired answers to questions asked by generals and heads of state. No matter that the counsel of the gods emerged in an inebriated garble; priests interpreted the oracular ravings and subdued them to intelligible words that often as not contained more ambiguity than straight advice.

Will the bird in the brushpile appear in plain sight? I put my question to an invisible oracle. The reply comes: Only if eyes are there to see, and even then, it depends on who keeps watch. Perhaps this isn't my day. Shall I stay or go back home? Suit yourself, and don't expect guidance from a figment of imagination.

A few more minutes of basking in sunshine, breathing the river-sweetened air, then we'll go. No signs of life now stir in the pile's stem-crowded recesses. The bird may have flown from its far side into the woods. There's plenty of winged action, though, on the pile's periphery. Today, no painted ladies try to assert dominance over one lone, brave, and tattered monarch, but I see a fluttering host—yellow sulphur butterflies, brown buckeyes with creamy eye-spots and orange embroidery on the upper wings, long-tailed skippers, the omnipresent swallowtails, including one Palamedes with wings of brown and yellow watered silk. Apart from the whirr of grasshoppers in the field and the whispers of breeze-brushed leaves, silence prevails. It's been an unusually quiet morning—few birdcalls from the underbrush, little fast-flying traffic in the upper stories of the trees around the field.

Oh. Hawk weather. A pale grey streak makes a low strafing run over the melon field. It's a male harrier. Mine haven't been the only watching eyes.

I rise and Sal bounds upright. She's back in her dervish mode, whirling in frenzied delight at the prospect of movement. I won't disappoint her by heading straight back to the trailer. We'll check the pond. The first of the wintering pied-billed grebes may have landed on its liquid acres. The arrival of ducks lies a full month away, but it's time for the little grebes. The brushpile is patient, will wait till tomorrow. So will the cherry tomatoes.

Tripod on shoulder, I turn my back on the Point's best brushpile and leave. Goose bumps rise light on the nape of my neck. Something seems to be watching, not songbird nor hawk but—I don't know. Something as reclusive as a little bird, but larger, even more teasing, more elemental. Sal cheers me on with crisp barks as I leap and spin around, laughing.

No grebe at the pond, but there is an otter.

Morning dawns fair, a welcome rerun of yesterday—the lightest breath of wind, full sun to bake off dew and the day's early chill, to provide the kind of light that glorifies color rather than demeans it. Of course, we're bound for the brushpile.

Oh my! In this garden that's grown like Topsy, amid its leaves and briers, glowing flowers and plump berries, from rooted stalks to topmost twigs—a riot of movement, a soft rain of noise. The commotion ceases for only a minute as dog and woman draw near. As soon as Sal hares off in the woods and I'm settled on my nonoracular tripod, it rises anew. Mockingbird gives me the raspberry, squawking full blast from a high branch. Five—no, six—cardinals play musical perches amid the pokeberries. Just over my head, a flapping of wings, and a seventh joins them. Two catbirds emerge from concealing greenery and, cocking their heads, eye me with curiosity. At ground level, a house wren pops out as if interrupted at some important task; its scolding call sizzles with indignation. And warblers are here, one male black-throated blue pausing in migration, a couple of yellow-rumps homing in for the winter, and another migrant, a young redstart, flitting around the cherry tomatoes and flashing two golden half-moon patches as it fans its tail. Never before have I seen a redstart so near the ground; its species prefers the more ethereal elevations. And in the woods that cup the field and its high-rise central garden, chickadees, towhees, a thrasher, a red-bellied woodpecker. Raucous squadrons of migrating blue jays streak overhead.

To watch and listen is to sit back making sociological notes on a popular resort, with lots of traffic, tourists coming and going, the natives pretty much tending to their own affairs, except for the mockingbird, which makes aggressive passes at those it deems unsuitable invaders of its self-proclaimed private spaces. But the analogy is not truly apt; it tries to cram wildness into a cage built of purely human terms and understanding. If anything's caged, it's I, caught in a separate awareness that can never apprehend what it is to be mockingbird, swallowtail, or beauty berry. Amid the robustious or restrained energies of flora and fauna, I sit here with—but not of—them. Outside the gates, I look back at Eden. All that my longing can do is ask questions. Myths and suppositions answer. Yet today I feel almost included in the action. I might put a hand through the barrier that stands between me and Paradise. The barrier is not a solid wall but an airy mesh.

Why do the birds show no fear this morning? Partly, I'm sure, because no keen yellow eyes, no hooked bill, no talons lurk in patient, predatory wait. The birds are well-attuned to my presence, though—the mocker sassing, the catbirds clearly inquisitive. Perhaps, after yesterday's hawk alert made them seek cover, they're just plain hungry and making up for a day of fasting. The crops in their islanded garden are superabundantly ready for harvest. Gorge while the gorging's good? Their boldness is a puzzle: I have sat here under circumstances apparently identical to those granted now—and birds glimpsed as I've trekked across the field have vanished absolutely. Silence. Stillness. Neither my eyes nor my intuition received the slightest hints that any bird remained even in the brushpile's deepest crevices. Today, however, avian work and play are being conducted at a high pitch of obviousness. Shall I take a risk?

To the uninitiated, people who watch birds may seem not quite right in the head. Not only do we stare for hours at nothing, we talk to it as well. But anticipation, if not sanity, lies behind such indications of madness. A short, sharp burst of applause may prod a clapper rail into loud, clattering response. The attention of chickadees and kinglets may be attracted by quick smacking kisses on the back of a hand. And there's no predicting what species may leave cover to check on the source of a reiterated *psssh*. Sometimes, however, the noises pique no avian interest. Instead, the birds hide or scatter, and nothing, not silence nor waiting, can coax them into sight.

"Psssh-psssh-psssh." The first to answer is Sally. She races around a corner and stops by my knees, then takes her boss position atop my feet. Experience has taught her that *psssh* is an oral command equivalent to *stay:* We won't be leaving this spot for a while, might as well lie down.

"Psssh-psssh-psssh." The mocker leaps to a higher branch and utters a loud blast; the cardinals pelt me with a sudden racket of dry, chipping calls; the house wren pops out again positively sputtering. And out of nowhere, a gift appears, a new bird for the day—ruby-crowned kinglet. It hovers like a slightly overweight hummingbird above the goldenrod. All's right with the world. The birds seem to recognize benignity, mine and that of everything else. The brush-pile's guardian, its tutelary spirit, has given them the go-ahead.

The presence sensed yesterday—if I were an ancient Greek or Roman, I would know without the least doubt whatsoever that divinity dwelled here. I'd know that the prickles on the back of my neck, the merriment that lifted me off my feet and whirled me around were acts of involuntary homage. Once upon an archaic time, the manifestations of nature, both living and inert, were understood to be the temporal houses for the energies of a realm in which all is eternal, interchangeable, and utterly immune to mortal strictures and inhibitions. The early Roman mind gave no particular shape to these intangible forces. The Greeks invested them with femininity, called them nymphs, and envisioned them as young women who presided within the existences of the things they inhabited, who sometimes left their allotted homes to dance or run errands for the gods. The nereids that dwelled in the oceans played with dolphins, escorted ships, and brought to earth the armor wrought in heaven for Achilles, hero of the Trojan War. Fresh waters—lakes, rivers, springs—gave shelter to naiads. Oreads animated hills and mountains. Every tree in the woods was home to a dryad. And all these nymphs were immortal except for the last. As the seed sprouted, its dryad would put down her own roots, thrust her own arms into light, leaf out, and grow, sap rising every spring, leaves fluttering earthward every fall, but when her tree died, toppled by age or lightning or an axe, she did not take refuge in another home but also died. (Across the millennia, I hear the cry of a proto-conservationist: "Woodsman, spare that tree!") If the mythological dictum that dryads must die while other nymphs keep going on forever seems grossly discriminatory, the reason may be that people concocted the myths, and people thought that they glimpsed an exemption from finitude in rocks and water, that mountains would always stand, the rivers and oceans flow without cease. But the lives of trees, like human lives, are measured in short years.

Fancy waves its magic wand: Let there be a dryad in the brush-pile! And why not? Of all the nymphs, only oreads scant this flat coast where all rocks have long been ground into grains of sand or the even finer components of clay. But nereids wearing bright scales and hair of green eelgrass gambol in the salty river, naiads disguised as otters frisk in the pond. Even the puddle on the pond road seems to have a guardian that watches over eastern mud turtles and baby snappers, leopard frogs and water striders, for the puddle never dries up entirely; when water disappears, the mud remains deep and moist, affording protection to adults and eggs alike. Of course, a dryad stands watch in the brushpile! Her aspect this morning is gaiety. She's decked out in a robe richly embroidered with leaves, flowers, feathers; her necklaces and rings are jeweled berries. Her smile shines bright and warm as the morning sun. And out of no-where, another gift: I understand that her presence here is not en-tirely a product of wishful thinking. No matter where she and her myriad sisters may be thought to dwell, in limestone or wood or rippling stream, they all personify an idea that's as real as a beauty berry or a pail of river water—the idea that all creation is due respect and not a little reverence.

"Psssh-psssh-psssh." The bustle in the brushpile does not abate. If anything, it intensifies: a towhee, a second black-throated blue warbler, a Carolina wren, and something that I've not seen at the Point before. Bigger than the wren, smaller than the towhee, it perches on a poke stem and obliges me by staying put for a full minute. Dark head and back, clear yellow breast and throat, white spectacles around its eyes—how splendid, a chat! I've expected to see one here sooner or later; these jumbo warblers breed in the county immediately to the south, most likely in this one as well, and loudly proclaim their territorial rights from the springtime treetops. Their talkative repertoire mingles clear whistles and soft caws with noises akin to those of a clanking machine or an unoiled hinge. I thank the dryad, fold my sit-upon, and leave.

The cherry tomatoes still hang on the vine. No grebe yet swims on the pond, its tiny wake drawing a thin, dark line across the water's silvered surface. The naiad-otters play somewhere else. But Sal gets fussed at by a marsh wren, and I succeed at clapping out a rail.

The sense of a tutelary presence persists. Call it numen—a shimmering, pulsing energy that rises from and enfolds a thousand thousand small lives and is greater than the sum of these parts because it includes not only past and present but the future as well. Within its compass, actuality is wedded to boundless potential.

Awareness of numen accompanies me on subsequent visits to the brushpile. By the first week in October, the pokeweed is denuded, leaves fallen, the last berry stripped, the purple-red stalks beginning to shrivel. Birds turn attention to the seedheads on flowers and grasses, to the clusters of electric beauty berries. The chat is gone—it lingered for a week—and so are the black-throated blues, but song and white-throated sparrows have moved in. Twice, on quiet days when birds were lying low or busy elsewhere, I've picked a pint of cherry tomatoes—sun candy, bursting with sugar and heat.

Numen invests the pond, too—the lone grebe that comes in on October first, the pair of wigeon observed a day later, the constant otters. It sways behind Mo's barn in the unmowed savannah of weeds where cottontails and cardinals thrive. It flutters with a flock of golden-crowned kinglets in the upper stories of the pines and with a solitary vireo in the unkempt shrubbery on the fringe of a neighbor's yard. It bounces off the river like reflected sunlight and squeals with the voice of a ring-billed gull or makes foghorn lament with the great black-backs. Like a scamper of sanderlings, it chases the frothy waves rolling in at the beach. It calls from a nighttime loblolly outside the trailer. In the cool morning, we find a great horned owl's feather at the foot of the deck steps.

I walk through October into November. Everywhere, from brushpile to barn to beach, my invisible companion tags along like a second dog, a stray, sometimes coming almost close enough to scratch behind the ears, more often skittering into the underbrush the moment I turn to face it. Numen—always, a small but unbridgeable distance lies between us. Always, I seem to be on the outside looking in—not a worthless place to be, a rewarding place in fact, kaleidoscopic with color, sounds, and movements, but also one that's faintly shadowed by a longing for something lost, for a homeland from which I and my kind are barred. What is humanity's role in regard to the sprawling brushpiles of the world and to its clearings, both those that are natural and those that result from the bulldozings of an awful mess? We seem to be exiled in perpetuity from the world's heart. And Western culture provides a metaphor: the expulsion from Eden. It is as if, after everything else was not only created but made complete, a pair of defiant upstarts were cut loose and told to go finish themselves.

Judaeo-Christian tradition palliates such bleakness by offering the exiles a choice between two roles. One, held out like a tempting apple in the very first chapter of Genesis, is that of dominion: "Then God said, 'Let us make man in our image and likeness to rule the fish of the sea, the birds of heaven, the cattle, all wild animals on earth, and all reptiles that crawl upon the earth.' " Two verses later, the commission to rule is repeated and augmented by another assignment—that Adam fill the earth and subdue it. The other role, offered in Genesis's second chapter, is that of stewardship: "The Lord God took the man and put him in the garden of Eden to till it and care for it." But both these hand-me-down models, venerable though they be, seem to lack something crucial. Dominion calls for the exercise of absolute control. The notion grinds earth under its booted heel. Stewardship is the gentler choice, the one that suggests a responsible parent. Its catch is that it licenses nurture for things that seem humanly desirable, but be damned with the rest. I cannot be satisfied with either model, for both place humankind behind a fence. Both decree our disconnectedness, our separation from the intricate tangle of everything else. In both, the habitat for numen dwindles.

What do I want? The whole works, that's all. Connections. Fusion. Blood ties. Oneness with the rest of creation.

I turn to the Greeks for help. They offer other lenses through which to view the human situation. Oracles? No. Woozy with bay leaves and ambiguity, they can stay on their tripods. I consult instead the plays of Aeschylus and Pindar's poems, singing to this day from the far edge of the fifth century B.C. They point back to an earlier belief that creation was originally seamless, that heaven and earth, the sacred and the quotidian, gods and creatures, all coexisted in the same unfrayed realm and from the beginning enjoyed a perfect equilibrium. Lions lay down with lambs; mortals supped at the tables of the gods; everyone minded the rules for good manners. Enter hybris, a holier-than-thou jab at the status quo. The scales tilt, and great gaping holes appear in the fabric. Aeschylus, the tragic poet, sees the severance between the timeless and the temporal as never to be healed. But Pindar, poet of festal sublimity, offers us hope in the dancing songs he composed to celebrate victories in major athletic contests, such as those held at Olympia to honor Zeus and at Delphi in Apollo's praise. Yes, he shouts, seamlessness may be regained, if only for fleeting, delirious moments. And joy is the instrument by which it's achieved. In the instant of victory—not in the running of a race, not in the later wave of public adulation that crashes over the winner, but in the brief moment of triumph as the finish line is crossed—joy turns the leaves of the victor's crown into real wings that literally lift him off the ground and place him for a split second into the arms of the unity that otherwise glimmers just beyond our mortal ken. And in that flash of time that is not time, anything is possible—dead ancestors wake at the hubbub and rejoice; history and myth mingle; past, present, and future slide together, forming a cohesive whole in which no part can be distinguished from the others.

Who is immune to joy? It may be won through events other than athletic triumph. Nor need it be strenuously sought and earned. Sometimes it sneaks up and looks for all the world exactly like a yellow-breasted chat. But the problem with joy as a means to oneness is that joy is evanescent. It gleams like a rainbow and just as quickly fades. And its briefness is a blessing, for the human body cannot long endure being kept in the air by a hyperkinetic pitch of elation. Biological necessity dictates the descent to earth. Joy, though welcome, is not a way of life.

It is the tragic poet, the man mortally sure that severance is incurable, who presents a modus vivendi. In play after play, he advocates striving for *kairos*—balance, moderation, a trading of hybris for humility. Step softly, he says, walk with measured tread among the world's perceptible phenomena, for every rock, tree, and river is the temporal home of some invisible and holy force that insists on reverence. But, if reverence is given short shrift or denied, down comes heaven's destroying fist.

Good for Aeschylus! He believes in dryads. And the principle of *kairos* seems fit and right. It accepts the loss of Eden and posits a method for dealing with the thorns outside the forever barred gates. In the same breath, however, it seems to place humanity at the bottom of creation's pecking order. No creatures but ourselves attract the hooked bill, the huge talons of divine wrath. We're still caged in separateness, still divided from brushpiles and birds, fish, cattle, and snakes. I stand here frustrated, rattling the bars.

November. The bars spread apart—not much but enough to allow light to strike from an unexpected angle. Cherry blossoms and jade-green moss, a pebble, a frog in a little pool—how delicate the instruments that make this opening.

A windy afternoon, and I've come to Morehead City to indulge my passion for acquiring books: a standard field guide to mushrooms, a just-published paperback about the coast's troubled waters, the latest Dr. Seuss to read to my granddaughter when she visits. Through the bookstore's plate-glass window, between and beyond the low-rise restaurants and boutiques, a view of Bogue Sound, breeze-whipped water grey under a sky of scudding clouds. Three head boats, fifty-foot inboards that cater to folks wanting to cast a line and catch a fish, rock massively at moorings that nose the tethered bows almost up to the edge of the macadam street. The street is packed with bumper-to-bumper parked cars and bordered by concrete sidewalks. The near sidewalk, one wide enough for three people to walk abreast with plenty of arm-swinging room, also makes room for a row of neat, head-high trees that screen off some of the cars but do not block the calm sight of sky, clouds, and salt water. The trees are hollies, not a native species but an import, scarlet berries pendant among thick, glossy leaves, but the leaves have no prickles and the mass of foliage atop each slender trunk looks as if some municipal topiary artist has trimmed it into a big green ball. No, the perfect roundness springs from the tree itself. Amid concrete and salt air, the town provides shelter for urban dryads. It's not a dryad, however, who pauses beside one holly. A short, skinny, raggedy man with weather-browned face and thinning salt-and-pepper hair stops, reaches toward a cluster of berries, plucks them, and drops them to the circle of concrete-walled earth beneath the tree. Passersby don't faze him in the least. He works till every last berry from his chosen tree lies on the ground. Then he moves on.

Shaking her head but smiling, the bookstore's manager says, "Don't know what possesses him. He does that all the time." Not the act but its chutzpah elicits her reluctant admiration. An exercise of dominion, I think, unwitting, but dominion nonetheless.

A hand on my shoulder, a hearty voice. "Good to see you!" It's a neighbor, a man who lives near the Point—ten miles by road, only two and a half by water. He's built the first house in a private development, recently surveyed and staked out into three hundred inland and waterfront lots, for which there will soon be provided such amenities as a clubhouse and a guard at the entrance gate. He's proud of his new home, tickled pink at its location on Clubfoot Creek. I relish his pleasure in the live oaks and native yaupon hollies, the pelicans and cooter turtles and jumping mullet that also much please me. It's not at all his fault that a good many land developers, including the one who sold him his lot, hold diplomas from the dominion school, that they practice a creeping, relentless tidiness, reducing disorderly wilderness to snaggle-stumped clearings. Under such conditions, brushpiles and their vivifying spirits have no chance. Unnatural succession takes hold—lo, stump grinders, tillers, well-trimmed borders, weedless lawns. The lots are not sterile, but they're surely sanitized to the picky specifications that only human beings can think up. I'd rather see discreet untidiness and berries left on the holly tree.

Our neighbor is accompanied by his wife, a woman well endowed with grace and a sparkling smile. She says, "We have a good, long-time friend visiting from Virginia. I'd like you to meet him."

Suddenly—blossoms, pebble, pool and frog, Bogue Sound, head boats, hollies, the browsers in the bookstore, the books at my elbow, in my hand, all disappear. I am swept into conversation. No, not conversation but listening to, trying to take in, a near monologue. The speaker's tone is matter-of-fact, his words intense. I am stunned. Joy lifts me off the ground.

My neighbors' guest has been introduced as Eli Takesian, a retired Navy chaplain who now ministers to a congregation in northern Virginia. A dark, wiry man, he shakes my hand and regards me with deep brown eyes that seem to be filled with post-Edenic sadness. Talk begins harmlessly enough with the usual extension of feelers for topics of mutual interest—my own affiliation with a retired Navy man, his appreciation for his hosts' new home and its lively river, its verdant landscape.

Then: "Of all types of gardens, the Japanese move me most."

And he tells of a book he treasures, one that treats of Japanese gardens and the ways in which they give resonant visual illustrations to a concept largely absent in the Western world. "You're familiar, of course, with the two stories of Genesis," he says. "Both of them license appropriation, possession. We're placed outside the natural process and given leave to whip it into shape or contain it within arbitrary bounds. The Japanese see man as part of nature, an element securely tucked within the whole." And quietly he expands upon this astonishing statement. The volume of which he speaks is now out of print, but before he leaves the bookstore, he promises a photocopy of its introduction and takes my address.

Dizzy, spun round one hundred eighty degrees, given a brand-new orientation, I drive home. My cage looks like an accident of Western perception.

December. Mountains on either hand, the Blue Ridge and the Western Range of the Appalachians—I cannot see them from where I sit, but they rise weathered, tree-clad, constant in mind's eye. What I do see from the kitchen window is this: two-level backyard dug out of a steep hillside—slippery elms with naked branches on the upper terrace, and on the lower, shaggy, frost-burned grass, spirea and rose of Sharon sprawling in untidy hibernation along the chain-link fence, a two-year-old Autumn Blaze pear tree still clutching one bronzed leaf, a Norway spruce lifting its green branches

toward the pale sky like a winner lifting arms to greet the adoring
crowd. And there is a crowd. Cardinals peck at rose-of-Sharon seed-
pods, juncos search the ground, house sparrows play tag in the
spirea, a host of house finches squabble about which gets a place on
one of the tubular feeder's six perches. The male finches look
drenched with raspberry juice. The flock scatters up, up, up to the
twigs of the slippery elms when the Chief goes out to restock the
feeder with sunflower seeds. When he comes back in, the finches
don't return immediately to the fray, for a red-bellied woodpecker
flies in and keeps off the noisy mob till it has pecked at and scattered
a third of the seeds.

The Point and its fluent river are temporarily abandoned. Like
wrong-way migrants, the Chief, Sally, and I have sped north along
the interstates to the Shenandoah Valley. As the year gathers darkness and cold in its slide toward the winter solstice, I am pulled back
to the town of my childhood by holidays—savory Thanksgiving,
Christmas fragrant with spices and resin. Here my family lives, and
four generations, from sprightly great-grandmother to goggle-eyed
babies, pack themselves into one or another of our houses for feasts
and laughter, presents and hugs. I cannot forgo this annual fix of
cozy, tribal heat. The river will wait.

With glee, I jump into the season like a child cannonballing into
a pool. Visits, cards, decorations, gifts to make and wrap, pies to be
baked of butternut squash that the Chief grew last summer at the
Point—the days and nights are caught up in rituals of celebration
that leave little time for anything else. The one respite is regular
walks in the woods with Sally so that she can stretch her long
Doberlegs, going ten miles to my one, as I look for birds, some of
them species not present at Great Neck Point—ruffed grouse, wild
turkeys.

And Christmas is coming, the geese are getting fat, please to put
a penny in an old man's hat: We drop coins into the Salvation Army
kettle outside the grocery story. O Christmas tree, O Christmas tree,
how lovely are thy branches. The Chief brings home a cut-it-
yourself, short-needled Tannenbaum that smells as sweet as Carolina piney woods. Hark, the herald angels sing. The crèche—some
of its figures, a cow, a camel, the pink plaster angel, as old as I
am—to be taken from its swaddlings of tissue paper and placed on

the mantel. The Christmas occasion sweeps me into its caroling embrace. More truly, however, I celebrate far older things—the circulating warmth of blood ties, the coming of the solstice that tilts earth's northern regions away from darkness toward the light, toward burgeoning and summer.

And in the season of affirmation, the envelope arrives, silent as a snowflake. I have completely forgotten Eli's promise, but he has not. Here, in my hand, are four pages. For an hour, festivities, finches, and mountains disappear. I'm watching the brushpile.

There are only two attitudes toward nature. One confronts it or one accepts it.

. . . The Western garden represents ambition attained, nature subdued. It is an illustration of the humanist ideal: man is the measure of all things.

The Eastern garden and its assumptions are quite different. Man finally and firmly becomes a part of nature itself. There is no assumption that there is something better than nature. Nature is itself and that is enough. . . . The man who can accept nature can also accept himself.

The words are those of Teiji Ito, and the book they introduce is *The Japanese Garden: An Approach to Nature*, published by Yale University in 1972. Only three and a half pages, but the concepts thereon are presented with the tightly coiled and powerful economy of a poem. I am told that acceptance of self is also acceptance of individual finitude. Yet, paradoxically, through such acceptance, time can be made to stop, for mortal flesh "has found a way to freeze it, suspend it, make it permanent . . . by letting it have its own way." The Japanese garden gives concrete expression to this sensibility by mingling components that blossom and wither with elements that are changeless and everlasting. Flowers and frog respond to the seasons amid immutable stones and ponds. (Dryads amid their imperishable sisters!) It is the gardener's task to release the beauty of the garden, not to create it. Nor might he dare hope to create beauty; to do so is not in his gift, for beauty does not exist as an abstraction unconnected to an object. Beauty is not ideal or potential but as actual and available to the senses as sap or flecks of mica. And,

. . . The garden lives. It grows, it changes. By incorporating into it the idea of change, the idea even of death, it triumphs over death itself—it is alive.

In an appended note, Eli issues a caveat: "To confront or accept *in extreme* can be problematic. The middle, moderate, balanced path ('the Golden Mean') is probably the best to walk."

But along with cautionary words, in this season of giving comes a gift of freedom. An unlatching of my cage's invisible door. A chance for seamlessness amid the obvious fractures of the world. I and my kind are as much a part of the whole as everything else—fish, birds, cattle, all wild creatures, all snakes, every apple within the gates, every thorn without. Mortality is remedied—canceled!—by the inclusion of the finite within the on-rolling, timeless process of growth and change. When one dryad falls, another takes her place, and another, another. The fact of change is unchangeable.

I'm still in the cage, though, despite its open door. Conventional wisdom is not easy to shake off. The habit of separateness is hard to unlearn. And the twentieth century knows all too well that rivers and mountains, the two landscapes that inform my days, are not eternal but fully as temporal as human flesh. They just have a good bit more staying power.

God rest ye merry, let nothing ye dismay.

January. Wind whips the river into whitecaps. Behind a stern overcast the sun glimmers weakly, as if it were under water. Rain looks probable, but it's not falling yet. As soon as I reach for my jacket, Sal starts to bounce. Take it easy, I tell her. Boots, hat, scarf, gloves, binoculars, and sit-upon—hey, dog, it takes a little time for your person to bundle up.

The first, and lesser, objective is to leave the river, get out of that nose-nipping wind. The main goal, of course, is the brushpile and whatever it may hold. The field's dry stalks crunch beneath my feet as I dodge around fire ant hills. Last fall, the hills were crumbling domes that hugged the earth; now they've turned into towers, some nearly a foot high. And look! A yard from woods' edge, a small, bright, reddish-orange something balloons from the brown field. Trash? No, a mushroom shaped like a canopy supported on four slim poles; it turns out to be a columned stinkhorn, as rank in odor as its name suggests.

The brushpile sleeps, its glorious autumnal raiment worn out and shed like tattered rags. Nothing's left but a starkly linear crosshatching of stems and branches, and nothing signals the presence of creaturely life within this bare geometry. I sit nonetheless, sheltered here from the river's wind, and wait to see what happens.

The brushpile is itself and that is enough. It changes, grows, triumphs over the death of one part by thrusting up another. It is alive. And it is fragile, subject to a multitude of possibilities—natural succession, blight, herbicides, human whim. The bulldozer that shoved together its generating logs and earth could raze it in a wink of time. Yet, somewhere another brushpile would rise.

I try the thought another way: As an integral part of the natural process, as an organism firmly within the whole, I also grow, change, and triumph. I am myself—not mockingbird, monarch butterfly, nor brier—and that is enough.

Except, it's not enough. Of all nature's higgledy-piggledy parts, only my species has cognizance of possibility and thus lacks innocence. But lack of innocence does not automatically equate with guilt—unless we also lack an ethic for dealing with the huge, muddled cohort of everything else. It becomes therefore urgent to choose a stance. Inside or outside, acceptance or confrontation, which shall it be?

Inside, of course, and a heady feeling of coming home. Nor is acceptance an idle leaning back while something else takes care of the chores; it is not devoid of responsibility. Like the Japanese gardener who wields his pruning shears not to trim a garden to some human notion of rightness but to release its inherent beauty and rejoice therein, I am commissioned not to trample but to enhance. Do unto others as you would have others do unto you. Let "others" include the four-footed critters, and those with six or eight legs, and those with no legs at all. Let it embrace every plant, all rocks, all water. And may there also be a habitat for numen, a shivering sense of something larger than oneself. The Golden Rule might also be radically rephrased: Do unto all others, animate or not, as you would do unto yourself. Now, that has a ring of ecological morality.

And there's Eli's gleaming reminder of the Golden Mean. We're back to *kairos*. The Greeks were right after all, and I was wrong to interpret the concept as divisive. It warns against puffing up self as the only animal fit for the top of the totem pole, but nowhere does it hint that our place is at the bottom. Nor does it deny that we ourselves might house numinous forces. All it does is enjoin us quite straightforwardly to walk between the vines, not on them.

Whee! But, damn, it's cold sitting here in the field. My toes are freezing. High time for dog and woman to take a brisk walk to the pond. But we don't go to the pond right away, nor does Sally care. All that's important to her is that we're moving at last. Impulse sends me instead to the edge of the woods where I pick up one end of a fallen but still green branch. Nothing visible inhabits the brush-pile this morning. So, there's nothing to disturb as I push the branch into the pile's center: in its decay, food for the plants and their dryad.

On the branches of a dormant beauty berry, buds have already begun to swell.

APPENDIX:

The Birds
of Great Neck Point

Red-throated loon, *Gavia stellata*
Common loon, *G. immer*
Pied-billed grebe, *Podilymbus podiceps*
Horned grebe, *Podiceps auritus*
American white pelican, *Pelecanus erythrorhynchos*
Brown pelican, *P. occidentalis*
Double-crested cormorant, *Phalacrocorax auritus*
Great blue heron, *Ardea herodias*
Great egret, *Casmerodius albus*

Snowy egret, *Egretta thula*
Little blue heron, *E. caerulea*
Tricolored heron, *E. tricolor*
Reddish egret, *E. rufescens*
Cattle egret, *Bubulcus ibis*
Green-backed heron, *Butorides striatus*
White ibis, *Eudocimus albus*
Glossy ibis, *Plegadis falcinellus*
Tundra swan, *Cygnus columbianus*
Snow goose, *Chen caerulescens*

Canada goose, *Branta canadensis*
Wood duck, *Aix sponsa*
Green-winged teal, *Anas crecca*
American black duck, *A. rubripes*
Mallard, *A. platyrhynchos*
Blue-winged teal, *A. discors*
Gadwall, *A. strepera*
American wigeon, *A. americana*
Canvasback, *Aythya valisineria*
Redhead, *A. americana*
Ring-necked duck, *A. collaris*
Greater scaup, *A. marila*
Lesser scaup, *A. affinis*
Oldsquaw, *Clangula hyemalis*
Black scoter, *Melanitta nigra*
Surf scoter, *M. perspicillata*
White-winged scoter, *M. deglandi*
Common goldeneye, *Bucephala clangula*
Bufflehead, *B. albeola*
Hooded merganser, *Lophodytes cucullatus*
Common merganser, *Mergus merganser*
Red-breasted merganser, *M. serrator*
Ruddy duck, *Oxyura jamaicensis*
Black vulture, *Coragyps atratus*
Turkey vulture, *Cathartes aura*
Osprey, *Pandion haliaetus*
Bald eagle, *Haliaeetus leucocephalus*
Northern harrier, *Circus cyaneus*
Sharp-shinned hawk, *Accipiter striatus*
Red-shouldered hawk, *Buteo Lineatus*
Broad-winged hawk, *B. platypterus*
Red-tailed hawk, *B. jamaicensis*
American kestrel, *Falco sparverius*
Merlin, *F. columbarius*

Northern bobwhite, *Colinus virginianus*
Clapper rail, *Rallus longirostris*
Virginia rail, *R. limicola*
Common moorhen, *Gallinula chloropus*
American coot, *Fulica americana*
Black-bellied plover, *Pluvialis squatarola*
Wilson's plover, *Charadrius wilsonia*
Semipalmated plover, *C. semipalmatus*
Piping plover, *C. melodus*
Killdeer, *C. vociferus*
American oystercatcher, *Haematopus palliatus*
Greater yellowlegs, *Tringa melanoleuca*
Lesser yellowlegs, *T. flavipes*
Solitary sandpiper, *T. solitaria*
Willet, *Catoptrophorus semipalmatus*
Spotted sandpiper, *Actitis macularia*
Whimbrel, *Numenius phaeopus*
Ruddy turnstone, *Arenaria interpres*
Sanderling, *Calidris alba*
Semipalmated sandpiper, *C. pusilla*
Least sandpiper, *C. minutilla*
Dunlin, *C. alpina*
Short-billed dowitcher, *Limnodromus griseus*
Common snipe, *Gallinago gallinago*
American woodcock, *Scolopax minor*
Red-necked phalarope, *Phalaropus lobatus*

Laughing gull, *Larus atricilla*
Bonaparte's gull, *L. philadelphia*
Ring-billed gull, *L. delawarensis*
Herring gull, *L. argentatus*
Great black-backed gull, *L. marinus*
Black-legged kittiwake, *Rissa tridactyla*
Caspian tern, *Sterna caspia*
Royal tern, *S. maxima*
Common tern, *S. hirundo*
Forster's tern, *S. forsteri*
Least tern, *S. antillarum*
Black skimmer, *Rhynchops niger*
Rock dove, *Columba livia*
Mourning dove, *Zenaida macroura*
Yellow-billed cuckoo, *Coccyzus americanus*
Eastern screech owl, *Otus asio*
Great horned owl, *Bubo virginianus*
Barred owl, *Strix varia*
Common nighthawk, *Chordeiles minor*
Chuck-will's-widow, *Caprimulges carolinensis*
Chimney swift, *Chaetura pelagica*
Ruby-throated hummingbird, *Archilochus colubris*
Belted kingfisher, *Ceryle alcyon*
Red-headed woodpecker, *Melanerpes erythrocephalus*
Red-bellied woodpecker, *M. carolinus*
Yellow-bellied sapsucker, *Sphyrapicus varius*
Downy woodpecker, *Picoides pubescens*
Hairy woodpecker, *P. villosus*
Northern flicker, *Colaptes auratus*

Pileated woodpecker, *Dryocopus pileatus*
Eastern wood-peewee, *Contopus virens*
Acadian flycatcher, *Empidonax virescens*
Eastern phoebe, *Sayornis phoebe*
Great crested flycatcher, *Myiarchus crinitus*
Western kingbird, *Tyrannus verticalis*
Eastern kingbird, *T. tyrannus*
Grey kingbird, *T. dominiscensis*
Purple martin, *Progne subis*
Tree swallow, *Tachycineta bicolor*
Northern rough-winged swallow, *Stelgidopteryx serripennis*
Barn swallow, *Hirundo rustica*
Blue jay, *Cyanocitta cristata*
American crow, *Corvus brachyrhynchos*
Fish crow, *C. ossifragus*
Carolina chickadee, *Parus carolinensis*
Tufted titmouse, *P. bicolor*
Brown-headed nuthatch, *Sitia pusilla*
Brown creeper, *Certhia americana*
Carolina wren, *Thryothorus ludovicianus*
Winter wren, *Troglodytes troglodytes*
House wren, *T. aedon*
Long-billed marsh wren, *Cistothorus palustris*
Golden-crowned kinglet, *Regulus satrapa*
Ruby-crowned kinglet, *R. calendula*
Blue-grey gnatcatcher, *Polioptila caerula*

Eastern bluebird, *Sialia sialis*
Veery, *Catharus fuscescens*
Swainson's thrush, *C. ustulatus*
Hermit thrush, *C. guttatus*
Wood thrush, *Hylocichla mustelina*
American robin, *Turdus migratorius*
Grey catbird, *Dumatella carolinensis*
Northern mockingbird, *Mimus polyglottos*
Brown thrasher, *Toxostoma rufus*
Cedar waxwing, *Bombycilla cedrorum*
European starling, *Sturnus vulgaris*
White-eyed vireo, *Vireo griseus*
Solitary vireo, *V. solitarius*
Yellow-throated vireo, *V. flavifrons*
Philadelphia vireo, *V. philadelphicus*
Red-eyed vireo, *V. olivaceus*
Orange-crowned warbler, *Vermivora celata*
Nashville warbler, *V. ruficapilla*
Northern parula, *Parula americana*
Yellow warbler, *Dendroica petechia*
Chestnut-sided warbler, *D. pensylvanica*
Cape May warbler, *D. tigrina*
Black-throated bue warbler, *D. caerulescens*
Yellow-rumped warbler, *D. coronata*
Black-throated green warbler, *D. virens*
Blackburnian warbler, *D. fusca*
Yellow-throated warbler, *D. dominica*
Pine warbler, *D. pinus*
Prairie warbler, *M. discolor*

Palm warbler, *D. palmarum*
Blackpoll warbler, *D. striata*
Black-and-white warbler, *Mniotilta varia*
American redstart, *Satophaga ruticilla*
Prothonotary warbler, *Protonotaria citrea*
Worm-eating warbler, *Helmitherus vermivorus*
Swainson's warbler, *Limnothlypis swainsonii*
Northern waterthrush, *Seiurus noveboracensis*
Common yellowthroat, *Geothlypsis trichas*
Hooded warbler, *Wilsonia citrina*
Wilson's warbler, *W. pusilla*
Yellow-breasted chat, *Icteria virens*
Summer tanager, *Piranga rubra*
Scarlet tanager, *P. olivacea*
Northern cardinal, *Cardinalis cardinalis*
Rose-breasted grosbeak, *Pheucticus ludovicianus*
Blue grosbeak, *Guiraca caerulea*
Indigo bunting, *Passerina cyanea*
Rufous-sided towhee, *Pipilo erythrophthalmus*
Chipping sparrow, *Spizella passerina*
Field sparrow, *S. pusilla*
Lark sparrow, *Chondestes grammacus*
Savannah sparrow, *Passerculus sandwichensis*
Grasshopper sparrow, *Ammodramus savannarum*
Fox sparrow, *Passerella iliaca*
Song sparrow, *Melospiza melodia*
Swamp sparrow, *M. georgiana*

White-throated sparrow, *Zonotrichia albicollis*

White-crowned sparrow, *Z. leucophrys*

Dark-eyed junco, *Junco hyemalis*

Bobolink, *Dolichonyx oryzivorus*

Red-winged blackbird, *Agelaius phoeniceus*

Eastern meadowlark, *Sturnella magna*

Boat-tailed grackle, *Quiscalus major*

Common grackle, *Q. quiscula*

Brown-headed cowbird, *Molothrus ater*

Orchard oriole, *Icterus spurius*

Northern oriole, *I. galbula galbula*

Purple finch, *Carpodacus purpureus*

House finch, *C. mexicanus*

American goldfinch, *Carduelis tristis*

Evening grosbeak, *Coccothraustes vespertinus*

House sparrow, *Passer domesticus*